Two Strike. *Frontispiece*
See page 152

INDIAN HEROES

AND

GREAT CHIEFTAINS

BY

CHARLES A. EASTMAN
(Ohiyesa)

University of Nebraska Press
Lincoln and London

First Bison Book printing: 1991
Most recent printing indicated by the last digit below:
10   9   8   7   6   5   4   3

Library of Congress Cataloging-in-Publication Data
Eastman, Charles Alexander, 1858–1939.
Indian heroes and great chieftains / by Charles A.
Eastman.
p. cm.
Reprint. Originally published: Boston: Little, Brown,
1918.
ISBN 0-8032-6720-7 (pa)
1. Indians of North America—Biography. 2. Dakota
Indians—Biography. I. Title.
E89.E13   1991
973'.0497022—dc20
[B]
90-21109   CIP

Originally published in 1918 by Little, Brown and
Company. Reprinted by arrangement with Mrs. Ernst
E. Mensel and Mrs. Virginia Whitbeck.

♾

CONTENTS

LIST OF PORTRAITS

INDIAN HEROES AND
GREAT CHIEFTAINS

RED CLOUD

EVERY age, every race, has its leaders
and heroes. There were over sixty
distinct tribes of Indians on this continent, each of which boasted its notable
men. The names and deeds of some of
these men will live in American history, yet
in the true sense they are unknown, because
misunderstood. I should like to present
some of the greatest chiefs of modern times
in the light of the native character and
ideals, believing that the American people
will gladly do them tardy justice.

It is matter of history that the Sioux
nation, to which I belong, was originally
friendly to the Caucasian peoples which it
met in succession — first, to the south the
Spaniards; then the French, on the Missis-

1

sippi River and along the Great Lakes;
later the English, and finally the Americans.
This powerful tribe then roamed over the
whole extent of the Mississippi valley, between that river and the Rockies. Their
usages and government united the various
bands more closely than was the case with
many of the neighboring tribes.

During the early part of the nineteenth
century, chiefs such as Wabashaw, Red-
wing, and Little Six among the eastern
Sioux, Conquering Bear, Man-Afraid-of-
His-Horse, and Hump of the western bands,
were the last of the old type. After these,
we have a coterie of new leaders, products
of the new conditions brought about by
close contact with the conquering race.

This distinction must be borne in mind
— that while the early chiefs were spokes-
men and leaders in the simplest sense,
possessing no real authority, those who
headed their tribes during the transition
period were more or less rulers and more or
less politicians. It is a singular fact that

many of the "chiefs", well known as such
to the American public, were not chiefs at
all according to the accepted usages of their
tribesmen. Their prominence was simply
the result of an abnormal situation, in
which representatives of the United States
Government made use of them for a definite
purpose. In a few cases, where a chief met
with a violent death, some ambitious man
has taken advantage of the confusion to
thrust himself upon the tribe and, perhaps
with outside help, has succeeded in usurping
the leadership.

Red Cloud was born about 1820 near the
forks of the Platte River. He was one of
a family of nine children whose father, an
able and respected warrior, reared his son
under the old Spartan régime. The young
Red Cloud is said to have been a fine horseman, able to swim across the Missouri and
Yellowstone rivers, of high bearing and un-
questionable courage, yet invariably gentle
and courteous in everyday life. This last
trait, together with a singularly musical and

agreeable voice, has always been characteristic of the man.

When he was about six years old, his father
gave him a spirited colt, and said to him :

"My son, when you are able to sit
quietly upon the back of this colt without
saddle or bridle, I shall be glad, for the boy
who can win a wild creature and learn to use
it will as a man be able to win and rule men."

The little fellow, instead of going for advice and help to his grandfather, as most
Indian boys would have done, began quietly
to practice throwing the lariat. In a little
while he was able to lasso the colt. He was
dragged off his feet at once, but hung on,
and finally managed to picket him near
the teepee. When the big boys drove the
herd of ponies to water, he drove his colt
with the rest. Presently the pony became
used to him and allowed himself to be
handled. The boy began to ride him bare-
back ; he was thrown many times, but persisted until he could ride without even a lariat,
sitting with arms folded and guiding the ani-

mal by the movements of his body. From that time on he told me that he broke all his own ponies, and before long his father's as well.

The old men, his contemporaries, have often related to me how Red Cloud was always successful in the hunt because his horses were so well broken. At the age of nine, he began to ride his father's pack pony upon the buffalo hunt. He was twelve years old, he told me, when he was first permitted to take part in the chase, and found to his great mortification that none of his arrows penetrated more than a few inches. Excited to recklessness, he whipped his horse nearer the fleeing buffalo, and before his father knew what he was about, he had seized one of the protruding arrows and tried to push it deeper. The furious animal tossed his massive head sidewise, and boy and horse were whirled into the air. Fortunately, the boy was thrown on the farther side of his pony, which received the full force of the second attack. The thundering hoofs of the stamped herd soon passed them by, but the wounded and maddened buffalo refused to move, and some critical moments passed before Red Cloud's father succeeded in attracting its attention so that the boy might spring to his feet and run for his life.

I once asked Red Cloud if he could recall having ever been afraid, and in reply he told me this story. He was about sixteen years old and had already been once or twice upon the warpath, when one fall his people were hunting in the Big Horn country, where they might expect trouble at any moment with the hostile Crows or Shoshones. Red Cloud had followed a single buffalo bull into the Bad Lands and was out of sight and hearing of his companions. When he had brought down his game, he noted carefully every feature of his surroundings so that he might at once detect anything unusual, and tied his horse with a long lariat to the horn of the dead bison, while skinning and cutting up the meat so as to pack it to camp. Every few minutes he paused in his work to scrutinize the landscape, for he had a feeling that danger was not far off.

Suddenly, almost over his head, as it seemed, he heard a tremendous war whoop, and glancing sidewise, thought he beheld the charge of an overwhelming number of warriors. He tried desperately to give the usual undaunted war whoop in reply, but instead a yell of terror burst from his lips, his legs gave way under him, and he fell in a heap. When he realized, the next instant, that the war whoop was merely the sudden loud whinnying of his own horse, and the charging army a band of fleeing elk, he was so ashamed of himself that he never forgot the incident, although up to that time he had never mentioned it. His subsequent career would indicate that the lesson was well learned.

The future leader was still a very young man when he joined a war party against the Utes. Having pushed eagerly forward on the trail, he found himself far in advance of his companions as night came on, and at the same time rain began to fall heavily. Among the scattered scrub pines, the lone warrior found a natural cave, and after a hasty examination, he decided to shelter there for the night.

Scarcely had he rolled himself in his blanket when he heard a slight rustling at the entrance, as if some creature were preparing to share his retreat. It was pitch dark. He could see nothing, but judged that it must be either a man or a grizzly. There was not room to draw a bow. It must be between knife and knife, or between knife and claws, he said to himself.

The intruder made no search but quietly lay down in the opposite corner of the cave. Red Cloud remained perfectly still, scarcely breathing, his hand upon his knife. Hour after hour he lay broad awake, while many thoughts passed through his brain. Suddenly, without warning, he sneezed, and instantly a strong man sprang to a sitting posture opposite. The first gray of morning was creeping into their rocky den, and behold ! a Ute hunter sat before him.

Desperate as the situation appeared, it was not without a grim humor. Neither could afford to take his eyes from the other's ; the tension was great, till at last a smile wavered over the expressionless face of the Ute. Red Cloud answered the smile, and in that instant a treaty of peace was born between them.

"Put your knife in its sheath. I shall do so also, and we will smoke together," signed Red Cloud. The other assented gladly, and they ratified thus the truce which assured to each a safe return to his friends. Having finished their smoke, they shook hands and separated. Neither had given the other any information. Red Cloud returned to his party and told his story, adding that he had divulged nothing and had nothing to report. Some were inclined to censure him for not fighting, but he was sustained by a majority of the warriors, who commended his self-restraint.

In a day or two they discovered the main camp of the enemy and fought a remarkable battle, in which Red Cloud especially distinguished himself.

The Sioux were now entering upon the most stormy period of their history. The old things were fast giving place to new. The young men, for the first time engaging in serious and destructive warfare with the neighboring tribes, armed with the deadly weapons furnished by the white man, began to realize that they must soon enter upon a desperate struggle for their ancestral hunting grounds. The old men had been innocently cultivating the friendship of the stranger, saying among themselves, "Surely there is land enough for all!"

Red Cloud was a modest and little known man of about twenty-eight years, when General Harney called all the western bands of Sioux together at Fort Laramie, Wyoming, for the purpose of securing an agreement and right of way through their territory. The Ogallalas held aloof from

this proposal, but Bear Bull, an Ogallala
chief, after having been plied with whisky,
undertook to dictate submission to the rest
of the clan. Enraged by failure, he fired
upon a group of his own tribesmen, and Red
Cloud's father and brother fell dead. According to Indian custom, it fell to him to
avenge the deed. Calmly, without uttering
a word, he faced old Bear Bull and his son,
who attempted to defend his father, and
shot them both. He did what he believed
to be his duty, and the whole band sustained him. Indeed, the tragedy gave the
young man at once a certain standing, as
one who not only defended his people
against enemies from without, but against
injustice and aggression within the tribe.
From this time on he was a recognized
leader.

Man-Afraid-of-His-Horse, then head chief
of the Ogallalas, took council with Red
Cloud in all important matters, and the
young warrior rapidly advanced in authority and influence. In 1854, when he

was barely thirty-five years old, the various bands were again encamped near Fort Laramie. A Mormon emigrant train, moving westward, left a footsore cow behind, and the young men killed her for food. The next day, to their astonishment, an officer with thirty men appeared at the Indian camp and demanded of old Conquering Bear that they be given up. The chief in vain protested that it was all a mistake and offered to make reparation. It would seem that either the officer was under the influence of liquor, or else had a mind to bully the Indians, for he would accept neither explanation nor payment, but demanded point-blank that the young men who had killed the cow be delivered up to summary punishment. The old chief refused to be intimidated and was shot dead on the spot. Not one soldier ever reached the gate of Fort Laramie! Here Red Cloud led the young Ogallalas, and so intense was the feeling that they even killed the half-breed interpreter.

Curiously enough, there was no attempt at retaliation on the part of the army, and no serious break until 1860, when the Sioux were involved in troubles with the Cheyennes and Arapahoes. In 1862, a grave outbreak was precipitated by the eastern Sioux in Minnesota under Little Crow, in which the western bands took no part. Yet this event ushered in a new period for their race. The surveyors of the Union Pacific were laying out the proposed road through the heart of the southern buffalo country, the rendezvous of Ogallalas, Brulés, Arapahoes, Comanches, and Pawnees, who followed the buffalo as a means of livelihood. To be sure, most of these tribes were at war with one another, yet during the summer months they met often to proclaim a truce and hold joint councils and festivities, which were now largely turned into discussions of the common enemy. It became evident, however, that some of the smaller and weaker tribes were inclined to welcome the new order of things, recognizing that it was the policy of the government to put an end to tribal warfare.

Red Cloud's position was uncompromisingly against submission. He made some noted speeches in this line, one of which was repeated to me by an old man who had heard and remembered it with the remarkable verbal memory of an Indian.

"Friends," said Red Cloud, "it has been our misfortune to welcome the white man. We have been deceived. He brought with him some shining things that pleased our eyes; he brought weapons more effective than our own : above all, he brought the spirit water that makes one forget for a time old age, weakness, and sorrow. But I wish to say to you that if you would possess these things for yourselves, you must begin anew and put away the wisdom of your fathers. You must lay up food, and forget the hungry. When your house is built, your storeroom filled, then look around for a neighbor whom you can take at a disadvantage, and seize all that he has !

Give away only what you do not want; or
rather, do not part with any of your possessions unless in exchange for another's.

"My countrymen, shall the glittering trin-
kets of this rich man, his deceitful drink
that overcomes the mind, shall these things
tempt us to give up our homes, our hunting
grounds, and the honorable teaching of our
old men? Shall we permit ourselves to be
driven to and fro — to be herded like the
cattle of the white man?"

His next speech that has been remembered was made in 1866, just before the
attack on Fort Phil Kearny. The tension
of feeling against the invaders had now
reached its height. There was no dissenting
voice in the council upon the Powder River,
when it was decided to oppose to the utter-
most the evident purpose of the government. Red Cloud was not altogether
ignorant of the numerical strength and the
resourcefulness of the white man, but he
was determined to face any odds rather
than submit.

"Hear ye, Dakotas!" he exclaimed. "When the Great Father at Washington sent us his chief soldier [General Harney] to ask for a path through our hunting grounds, a way for his iron road to the mountains and the western sea, we were told that they wished merely to pass through our country, not to tarry among us, but to seek for gold in the far west. Our old chiefs thought to show their friendship and good will, when they allowed this dangerous snake in our midst. They promised to protect the wayfarers.

"Yet before the ashes of the council fire are cold, the Great Father is building his forts among us. You have heard the sound of the white soldier's ax upon the Little Piney. His presence here is an insult and a threat. It is an insult to the spirits of our ancestors. Are we then to give up their sacred graves to be plowed for corn? Dakotas, I am for war!"

In less than a week after this speech, the Sioux advanced upon Fort Phil Kearny, the new sentinel that had just taken her place upon the farthest frontier, guarding the Oregon Trail. Every detail of the attack had been planned with care, though not without heated discussion, and nearly every well-known Sioux chief had agreed in striking the blow. The brilliant young war leader, Crazy Horse, was appointed to lead the charge. His lieutenants were Sword, Hump, and Dull Knife, with Little Chief of the Cheyennes, while the older men acted as councilors. Their success was instantaneous. In less than half an hour, they had cut down nearly a hundred men under Captain Fetterman, whom they drew out of the fort by a ruse and then annihilated.

Instead of sending troops to punish, the government sent a commission to treat with the Sioux. The result was the famous treaty of 1868, which Red Cloud was the last to sign, having refused to do so until all of the forts within their territory should be vacated. All of his demands were acceded to, the new road abandoned, the garrisons withdrawn, and in the new treaty it was distinctly stated that the Black Hills and the Big Horn were Indian country, set apart for their perpetual occupancy, and that no white man should enter that region without the consent of the Sioux.

Scarcely was this treaty signed, however, when gold was discovered in the Black Hills, and the popular cry was: "Remove the Indians!" This was easier said than done. That very territory had just been solemnly guaranteed to them forever: yet how stem the irresistible rush for gold? The government, at first, entered some small protest, just enough to "save its face", as the saying is; but there was no serious attempt to prevent the wholesale violation of the treaty. It was this state of affairs that led to the last great speech made by Red Cloud, at a gathering upon the Little Rosebud River. It is brief, and touches upon the hopelessness of their future as a race. He seems at about this time to have reached the conclusion that resistance could not

last much longer; in fact, the greater part
of the Sioux nation was already under
government control.

"We are told," said he, "that Spotted
Tail has consented to be the Beggars' Chief.
Those Indians who go over to the white
man can be nothing but beggars, for he
respects only riches, and how can an Indian
be a rich man? He cannot without ceasing
to be an Indian. As for me, I have listened
patiently to the promises of the Great
Father, but his memory is short. I am
now done with him. This is all I have to
say."

The wilder bands separated soon after
this council, to follow the drift of the
buffalo, some in the vicinity of the Black
Hills and others in the Big Horn region.
Small war parties came down from time to
time upon stray travelers, who received no
mercy at their hands, or made dashes upon
neighboring forts. Red Cloud claimed the
right to guard and hold by force, if need be,
all this territory which had been conceded

to his people by the treaty of 1868. **The**
land became a very nest of outlawry.
Aside from organized parties of prospectors,
there were bands of white horse thieves
and desperadoes who took advantage of the
situation to plunder immigrants and Indians
alike.

An attempt was made by means of
military camps to establish control and
force all the Indians upon reservations, and
another commission was sent to negotiate
their removal to Indian Territory, but met
with an absolute refusal. After much guer-
rilla warfare, an important military campaign against the Sioux was set on foot in
1876, ending in Custer's signal defeat upon
the Little Big Horn.

In this notable battle, Red Cloud did not
participate in person, nor in the earlier one
with Crook upon the Little Rosebud, but
he had a son in both fights. He was now
a councilor rather than a warrior, but his
young men were constantly in the field,
while Spotted Tail had definitely surren-

dered and was in close touch with representatives of the government.

But the inevitable end was near. One morning in the fall of 1876 Red Cloud was surrounded by United States troops under the command of Colonel McKenzie, who disarmed his people and brought them into Fort Robinson, Nebraska. Thence they were removed to the Pine Ridge agency, where he lived for more than thirty years as a "reservation Indian." In order to humiliate him further, government authorities proclaimed the more tractable Spotted Tail head chief of the Sioux. Of course, Red Cloud's own people never recognized any other chief.

In 1880 he appealed to Professor Marsh, of Yale, head of a scientific expedition to the Bad Lands, charging certain frauds at the agency and apparently proving his case; at any rate the matter was considered worthy of official investigation. In 1890–1891, during the "Ghost Dance craze" and the difficulties that followed, he was suspected of collusion with the hostiles, but he did not join them openly, and nothing could be proved against him. He was already an old man, and became almost entirely blind before his death in 1909 in his ninetieth year.

His private life was exemplary. He was faithful to one wife all his days, and was a devoted father to his children. He was ambitious for his only son, known as Jack Red Cloud, and much desired him to be a great warrior. He started him on the war-path at the age of fifteen, not then realizing that the days of Indian warfare were well-nigh at an end.

Among latter-day chiefs, Red Cloud was notable as a quiet man, simple and direct in speech, courageous in action, an ardent lover of his country, and possessed in a marked degree of the manly qualities characteristic of the American Indian in his best days.

JACK RED CLOUD, SON OF RED CLOUD

SPOTTED TAIL

A MONG the Sioux chiefs of the "transition period" only one was shrewd enough to read coming events in their true light. It is said of Spotted Tail that he was rather a slow-moving boy, preferring in their various games and mimic battles to play the rôle of councilor, to plan and assign to the others their parts in the fray. This he did so cleverly that he soon became a leader among his youthful contemporaries; and withal he was apt at mimicry and impersonation, so that the other boys were accustomed to say of him, "He has his grandfather's wit and the wisdom of his grandmother!"

Spotted Tail was an orphan, reared by his grandparents, and at an early age compelled to shift for himself. Thus he was somewhat at a disadvantage among the

other boys; yet even this fact may have
helped to develop in him courage and in-
genuity.   One little incident of his boy life,
occurring at about his tenth year, is characteristic of the man.   In the midst of a
game, two boys became involved in a dis-
pute which promised to be a serious one,
as both drew knives.   The young Spotted
Tail instantly began to cry, "The Shoshones are upon us!   To arms! to arms!"
and the other boys joined in the war whoop.
This distracted the attention of the com-
batants and ended the affair.

Upon the whole, his boyhood is not so
well remembered as is that of most of his
leading contemporaries, probably because
he had no parents to bring him frequently
before the people, as was the custom with
the well-born, whose every step in their
progress toward manhood was publicly
announced at a feast given in their honor.
It is known, however, that he began at an
early age to carve out a position for himself.
It is personal qualities alone that tell among

our people, and the youthful Spotted Tail
gained at every turn. At the age of seventeen, he had become a sure shot and a
clever hunter; but, above all, he had
already shown that he possessed a superior
mind. He had come into contact with
white people at the various trading posts,
and according to his own story had made a
careful study of the white man's habits and
modes of thought, especially of his peculiar
trait of economy and intense desire to
accumulate property. He was accustomed
to watch closely and listen attentively
whenever any of this strange race had dealings with his people. When a council was
held, and the other young men stood at a
distance with their robes over their faces
so as to avoid recognition, Spotted Tail
always put himself in a position to hear all
that was said on either side, and weighed
all the arguments in his mind.

When he first went upon the warpath, it
appears that he was, if anything, over-
zealous to establish himself in the eye of

his people; and as a matter of fact, it was especially hard for him to gain an assured position among the Brulés, with whom he lived, both because he was an orphan, and because his father had been of another band. Yet it was not long before he had achieved his ambition, though in doing so he received several ugly wounds. It was in a battle with the Utes that he first notably served his people and their cause.

The Utes were the attacking party and far outnumbered the Sioux on this occasion. Many of their bravest young men had fallen, and the Brulés were face to face with utter annihilation, when Spotted Tail, with a handful of daring horsemen, dodged around the enemy's flank and fell upon them from the rear with so much spirit that they supposed that strong reinforcements had arrived, and retreated in confusion. The Sioux pursued on horseback; and it was in this pursuit that the noted chief Two Strike gained his historical name. But the chief honors of the fight belonged

to Spotted Tail. The old chiefs, Conquering Bear and the rest, thanked him
and at once made him a war chief.

It had been the firm belief of Spotted
Tail that it was unwise to allow the white
man so much freedom in our country, long
before the older chiefs saw any harm in it.
After the opening of the Oregon Trail he,
above all the others, was watchful of the
conduct of the Americans as they journeyed
toward the setting sun, and more than once
he remarked in council that these white
men were not like the French and the
Spanish, with whom our old chiefs had been
used to deal. He was not fully satisfied
with the agreement with General Harney;
but as a young warrior who had only just
gained his position in the council, he could
not force his views upon the older men.

No sooner had the Oregon Trail been
secured from the Sioux than Fort Laramie
and other frontier posts were strengthened,
and the soldiers became more insolent and
overbearing than ever. It was soon dis-

covered that the whites were prepared to violate most of the articles of their treaty as the Indians understood it. At this time, the presence of many Mormon emigrants on their way to the settlements in Utah and Wyoming added to the perils of the situation, as they constantly maneuvered for purposes of their own to bring about a clash between the soldiers and the Indians. Every summer there were storm-clouds blowing between these two — clouds usually taking their rise in some affair of the travelers along the trail.

In 1854 an event occurred which has already been described and which snapped the last link of friendship between the races.

By this time Spotted Tail had proved his courage both abroad and at home. He had fought a duel with one of the lesser chiefs, by whom he was attacked. He killed his opponent with an arrow, but himself received upon his head a blow from a battle-axe which brought him senseless to the ground. He was left for dead, but fortunately revived just as the men were preparing his body for burial.

The Brulés sustained him in this quarrel, as he had acted in self-defense; and for a few years he led them in bloody raids against the whites along the historic trail. He ambushed many stagecoaches and emigrant trains, and was responsible for waylaying the Kincaid coach with twenty thousand dollars. This relentless harrying of travelers soon brought General Harney to the Brulé Sioux to demand explanations and reparation.

The old chiefs of the Brulés now appealed to Spotted Tail and his young warriors not to bring any general calamity upon the tribe. To the surprise of all, Spotted Tail declared that he would give himself up. He said that he had defended the rights of his people to the best of his ability, that he had avenged the blood of their chief, Conquering Bear, and that he was not afraid to accept the consequences. He therefore voluntarily surrendered to General Harney,

and two of his lieutenants, Red Leaf and
Old Woman, followed his example.

Thus Spotted Tail played an important
part at the very outset of those events
which were soon to overthrow the free life
of his people. I do not know how far he
foresaw what was to follow; but whether
so conceived or not, his surrender was a
master stroke, winning for him not only the
admiration of his own people but the confidence and respect of the military.

Thus suddenly he found himself in prison,
a hostage for the good behavior of his followers. There were many rumors as to the
punishment reserved for him; but luckily
for Spotted Tail, the promises of General
Harney to the Brulé chiefs in respect to him
were faithfully kept. One of his fellow-
prisoners committed suicide, but the other
held out bravely for the two-year term of
his imprisonment. During the second year,
it was well understood that neither of the
men sought to escape, and they were given
much freedom. It was fine schooling for

Spotted Tail, that tireless observer of the ways of the white man! It is a fact that his engaging personal qualities won for him kindness and sympathy at the fort before the time came for his release.

One day some Indian horse thieves of another tribe stampeded the horses and mules belonging to the garrison. Spotted Tail asked permission of the commanding officer to accompany the pursuers. That officer, trusting in the honor of a Sioux brave, gave him a fast horse and a good carbine, and said to him: "I depend upon you to guide my soldiers so that they may overtake the thieves and recapture the horses!"

The soldiers recaptured the horses without any loss, but Spotted Tail still followed the Indians. When they returned to the fort without him, everybody agreed that he would never turn up. However, next day he did "turn up", with the scalp of one of the marauders!

Soon after this he was returned to his own

people, who honored him by making him
the successor of the old chief, Conquering
Bear, whose blood he had avenged, for
which act he had taken upon himself the
full responsibility. He had made good use of
his two years at the fort, and completed his
studies of civilization to his own satisfaction.
From this time on he was desirous of
reconciling the Indian and the white man,
thoroughly understanding the uselessness
of opposition. He was accordingly in con-
stant communication with the military;
but the other chiefs did not understand his
views and seem to have been suspicious of
his motives.

In 1860–1864 the Southern Cheyennes
and Comanches were at war with the whites,
and some of the Brulés and Ogallalas, who
were their neighbors and intimates, were
suspected of complicity with the hostiles.
Doubtless a few of their young men may
have been involved; at any rate, Thunder
Bear and Two Face, together with a few
others who were roving with the warring

tribes, purchased two captive white women
and brought them to Fort Laramie. It
was, however, reported at the post that
these two men had maltreated the women
while under their care.

Of course, the commander demanded of
Spotted Tail, then head chief, that he give
up the guilty ones, and accordingly he had
the two men arrested and delivered at the
fort. At this there was an outcry among
his own people; but he argued that if the
charges were true, the men deserved punishment, and if false, they should be tried and
cleared by process of law. The Indians
never quite knew what evidence was pro-
duced at the court-martial, but at all events
the two men were hanged, and as they had
many influential connections, their relatives
lost no time in fomenting trouble. The
Sioux were then camping close by the fort
and it was midwinter, which facts held
them in check for a month or two; but as
soon as spring came, they removed their
camp across the river and rose in rebellion.

A pitched battle was fought, in which the soldiers got the worst of it. Even the associate chief, Big Mouth, was against Spotted Tail, who was practically forced against his will and judgment to take up arms once more.

At this juncture came the sudden and bloody uprising in the east among the Minnesota Sioux, and Sitting Bull's campaign in the north had begun in earnest; while to the south the Southern Cheyennes, Comanches, and Kiowas were all upon the warpath. Spotted Tail at about this time seems to have conceived the idea of uniting all the Rocky Mountain Indians in a great confederacy. He once said: "Our cause is as a child's cause, in comparison with the power of the white man, unless we can stop quarreling among ourselves and unite our energies for the common good." But old-time antagonisms were too strong; and he was probably held back also by his consciousness of the fact that the Indians called him "the white man's friend", while the military still had some faith in him which he did not care to lose. He was undoubtedly one of the brainiest and most brilliant Sioux who ever lived; and while he could not help being to a large extent in sympathy with the feeling of his race against the invader, yet he alone foresaw the inevitable outcome, and the problem as it presented itself to him was simply this: "What is the best policy to pursue in the existing situation?"

Here is his speech as it has been given to me, delivered at the great council on the Powder River, just before the attack on Fort Phil Kearny. We can imagine that he threw all his wonderful tact and personal magnetism into this last effort at conciliation.

"'Hay, hay, hay! Alas, alas!' Thus speaks the old man, when he knows that his former vigor and freedom is gone from him forever. So we may exclaim to-day, Alas! There is a time appointed to all things. Think for a moment how many multitudes of the animal tribes we ourselves have destroyed! Look upon the snow that appears to-day — to-morrow it is water! Listen to the dirge of the dry leaves, that were green and vigorous but a few moons before! We are a part of this life and it seems that our time is come.

"Yet note how the decay of one nation invigorates another. This strange white man — consider him, his gifts are manifold! His tireless brain, his busy hand do wonders for his race. Those things which we despise he holds as treasures; yet he is so great and so flourishing that there must be some virtue and truth in his philosophy. I wish to say to you, my friends: Be not moved alone by heated arguments and thoughts of revenge! These are for the young. We are young no longer; let us think well, and give counsel as old men!"

These words were greeted with an ominous silence. Not even the customary "How!" of assent followed the speech, and Sitting Bull immediately got up and replied in the celebrated harangue which will be introduced under his own name in another chapter. The situation was critical for Spotted Tail — the only man present to advocate submission to the stronger race whose ultimate supremacy he recognized as certain. The decision to attack Fort Phil Kearny was unanimous without him, and in order to hold his position among his tribesmen he joined in the charge. Several bullets passed through his war bonnet, and he was slightly wounded.

When the commission of 1867–1868 was sent out to negotiate with the Sioux, Spotted Tail was ready to meet them, and eager to obtain for his people the very best terms that he could. He often puzzled and embarrassed them by his remarkable speeches, the pointed questions that he put, and his telling allusions to former negotiations. Meanwhile Red Cloud would not come into the council until after several deputations of Indians had been sent to him, and Sitting Bull did not come at all.

The famous treaty was signed, and from

this time on Spotted Tail never again took up arms against the whites. On the contrary, it was mainly attributed to his influence that the hostiles were subdued much sooner than might have been expected. He came into the reservation with his band, urged his young men to enlist as government scouts, and assisted materially in all negotiations. The hostile chiefs no longer influenced his action, and as soon as they had all been brought under military control, General Crook named Spotted Tail head chief of the Sioux, thus humiliating Red Cloud and arousing jealousy and ill-feeling among the Ogallalas. In order to avoid trouble, he prudently separated himself from the other bands, and moved to the new agency on Beaver Creek (Fort Sheridan, Nebraska), which was called "Spotted Tail Agency."

Just before the daring war leader, Crazy Horse, surrendered to the military, he went down to the agency and roundly rebuked Spotted Tail for signing away the freedom

SPOTTED TAIL

of his people. From the point of view of
the irreconcilables, the diplomatic chief was
a "trimmer" and a traitor; and many of the
Sioux have tried to implicate him in the
conspiracy against Crazy Horse which led
to his assassination, but I hold that the
facts do not bear out this charge.

The name of Spotted Tail was promi-
nently before the people during the rest
of his life. An obscure orphan, he had
achieved distinction by his bravery and
sagacity; but he copied the white politician
too closely after he entered the reservation.
He became a good manipulator, and was
made conceited and overbearing by the
attentions of the military and of the general
public. Furthermore, there was an old
feud in his immediate band which affected
him closely. Against him for many years
were the followers of Big Mouth, whom he
had killed in a duel; and also a party led by
a son and a nephew of the old chief, Conquering Bear, whom Spotted Tail had succeeded at his death. These two men had

hoped that one or the other of them might obtain the succession.

Crow Dog, the nephew of Conquering Bear, more than once taunted Spotted Tail with the fact that he was chief not by the will of the tribe, but by the help of the white soldiers, and told him that he would "keep a bullet for him" in case he ever disgraced his high position. Thus retribution lay in wait for him while at the height of his fame. Several high-handed actions of his at this time, including his elopement with another man's wife, increased his unpopularity with a large element of his own tribe. On the eve of the chief's departure for Washington, to negotiate (or so they suspected) for the sale of more of their land, Crow Dog took up his gun and fulfilled his threat, regarding himself, and regarded by his supporters, not as a murderer, but as an executioner.

Such was the end of the man who may justly be called the Pontiac of the west. He possessed a remarkable mind and extraordinary foresight for an untutored savage; and yet he is the only one of our great men to be remembered with more honor by the white man, perhaps, than by his own people.

LITTLE CROW

CHIEF LITTLE CROW was the eldest son of Cetanwakuwa (Charging Hawk). It was on account of his father's name, mistranslated Crow, that he was called by the whites "Little Crow." His real name was Taoyateduta, His Red People.

As far back as Minnesota history goes, a band of the Sioux called Kaposia (Light Weight, because they were said to travel light) inhabited the Mille Lacs region. Later they dwelt about St. Croix Falls, and still later near St. Paul. In 1840, Cetanwakuwa was still living in what is now West St. Paul, but he was soon after killed by the accidental discharge of his gun.

It was during a period of demoralization for the Kaposias that Little Crow became the leader of his people. His father, a well-

known chief, had three wives, all from
different bands of the Sioux. He was the
only son of the first wife, a Leaf Dweller.
There were two sons of the second and two
of the third wife, and the second set of
brothers conspired to kill their half-brother
in order to keep the chieftainship in the
family.

Two kegs of whisky were bought, and
all the men of the tribe invited to a feast.
It was planned to pick some sort of quarrel
when all were drunk, and in the confusion
Little Crow was to be murdered. The plot
went smoothly until the last instant, when
a young brave saved the intended victim
by knocking the gun aside with his hatchet,
so that the shot went wild. However, it
broke his right arm, which remained crooked
all his life. The friends of the young
chieftain hastily withdrew, avoiding a general fight; and later the council of the
Kaposias condemned the two brothers,
both of whom were executed, leaving him
in undisputed possession.

Such was the opening of a stormy career.
Little Crow's mother had been a chief's
daughter, celebrated for her beauty and
spirit, and it is said that she used to plunge
him into the lake through a hole in the ice,
rubbing him afterward with snow, to
strengthen his nerves, and that she would
remain with him alone in the deep woods
for days at a time, so that he might know
that solitude is good, and not fear to be
alone with nature.

"My son," she would say, "if you are to
be a leader of men, you must listen in silence
to the mystery, the spirit."

At a very early age she made a feast for
her boy and announced that he would fast
two days. This is what might be called a
formal presentation to the spirit or God.
She greatly desired him to become a worthy
leader according to the ideas of her people.
It appears that she left her husband when
he took a second wife, and lived with her
own band till her death. She did not
marry again.

Little Crow was an intensely ambitious man and without physical fear. He was always in perfect training and early acquired the art of warfare of the Indian type. It is told of him that when he was about ten years old, he engaged with other boys in a sham battle on the shore of a lake near St. Paul. Both sides were encamped at a little distance from one another, and the rule was that the enemy must be surprised, otherwise the attack would be considered a failure. One must come within so many paces undiscovered in order to be counted successful. Our hero had a favorite dog which, at his earnest request, was allowed to take part in the game, and as a scout he entered the enemy camp unseen, by the help of his dog.

When he was twelve, he saved the life of a companion who had broken through the ice by tying the end of a pack line to a log, then at great risk to himself carrying it to the edge of the hole where his comrade went down. It is said that he also broke in, but both boys saved themselves by means of the line.

As a young man, Little Crow was always ready to serve his people as a messenger to other tribes, a duty involving much danger and hardship. He was also known as one of the best hunters in his band. Although still young, he had already a war record when he became chief of the Kaposias, at a time when the Sioux were facing the greatest and most far-reaching changes that had ever come to them.

At this juncture in the history of the northwest and its native inhabitants, the various fur companies had paramount influence. They did not hesitate to impress the Indians with the idea that they were the authorized representatives of the white races or peoples, and they were quick to realize the desirability of controlling the natives through their most influential chiefs. Little Crow became quite popular with post traders and factors. He was an orator as well as a diplomat, and one of the first of his

nation to indulge in politics and promote
unstable schemes to the detriment of his
people.

When the United States Government
went into the business of acquiring territory
from the Indians so that the flood of western
settlement might not be checked, commissions were sent out to negotiate treaties,
and in case of failure it often happened that
a delegation of leading men of the tribe were
invited to Washington. At that period,
these visiting chiefs, attired in all the
splendor of their costumes of ceremony,
were treated like ambassadors from foreign
countries.

One winter in the late eighteen-fifties, a
major general of the army gave a dinner to
the Indian chiefs then in the city, and on
this occasion Little Crow was appointed
toastmaster. There were present a number
of Senators and members of Congress, as
well as judges of the Supreme Court,
cabinet officers, and other distinguished
citizens. When all the guests were seated,

the Sioux arose and addressed them with much dignity as follows:

"Warriors and friends: I am informed that the great white war chief who of his generosity and comradeship has given us this feast, has expressed the wish that we may follow to-night the usages and customs of my people. In other words, this is a warriors' feast, a braves' meal. I call upon the Ojibway chief, the Hole-in-the-Day, to give the lone wolf's hunger call, after which we will join him in our usual manner."

The tall and handsome Ojibway now rose and straightened his superb form to utter one of the clearest and longest wolf howls that was ever heard in Washington, and at its close came a tremendous burst of war whoops that fairly rent the air, and no doubt electrified the officials there present.

On one occasion Little Crow was invited by the commander of Fort Ridgeley, Minnesota, to call at the fort. On his way back, in company with a half-breed named Ross and the interpreter Mitchell, he was am-

bushed by a party of Ojibways, and again
wounded in the same arm that had been
broken in his attempted assassination. His
companion Ross was killed, but he managed
to hold the war party at bay until help came
and thus saved his life.

More and more as time passed, this
naturally brave and ambitious man became
a prey to the selfish interests of the traders
and politicians. The immediate causes of
the Sioux outbreak of 1862 came in quick
succession to inflame to desperate action an
outraged people. The two bands on the
so-called "lower reservations" in Minnesota
were Indians for whom nature had provided
most abundantly in their free existence.
After one hundred and fifty years of
friendly intercourse first with the French,
then the English, and finally the Americans,
they found themselves cut off from every
natural resource, on a tract of land twenty
miles by thirty, which to them was virtual
imprisonment. By treaty stipulation with
the government, they were to be fed and

clothed, houses were to be built for them, the men taught agriculture, and schools provided for the children. In addition to this, a trust fund of a million and a half was to be set aside for them, at five per cent interest, the interest to be paid annually per capita. They had signed the treaty under pressure, believing in these promises on the faith of a great nation.

However, on entering the new life, the resources so rosily described to them failed to materialize. Many families faced starvation every winter, their only support the store of the Indian trader, who was baiting his trap for their destruction. Very gradually they awoke to the facts. At last it was planned to secure from them the north half of their reservation for ninety-eight thousand dollars, but it was not explained to the Indians that the traders were to receive all the money. Little Crow made the greatest mistake of his life when he signed this agreement.

Meanwhile, to make matters worse, the

cash annuities were not paid for nearly two
years. Civil War had begun. When it
was learned that the traders had taken all
of the ninety-eight thousand dollars "on
account", there was very bitter feeling.
In fact, the heads of the leading stores were
afraid to go about as usual, and most of
them stayed in St. Paul. Little Crow was
justly held in part responsible for the deceit,
and his life was not safe.

The murder of a white family near Acton,
Minnesota, by a party of Indian duck
hunters in August, 1862, precipitated the
break. Messengers were sent to every
village with the news, and at the villages of
Little Crow and Little Six the war council
was red-hot. It was proposed to take
advantage of the fact that north and south
were at war to wipe out the white settlers
and to regain their freedom. A few men
stood out against such a desperate step, but
the conflagration had gone beyond their
control.

There were many mixed bloods among

these Sioux, and some of the Indians held
that these were accomplices of the white
people in robbing them of their possessions,
therefore their lives should not be spared.
My father, Many Lightnings, who was
practically the leader of the Mankato band
(for Mankato, the chief, was a weak man),
fought desperately for the lives of the half-
breeds and the missionaries. The chiefs
had great confidence in my father, yet they
would not commit themselves, since their
braves were clamoring for blood. Little
Crow had been accused of all the mis-
fortunes of his tribe, and he now hoped by
leading them against the whites to regain
his prestige with his people, and a part at
least of their lost domain.

There were moments when the pacifists
were in grave peril. It was almost daybreak when my father saw that the ap-
proaching calamity could not be prevented.
He and two others said to Little Crow: "If
you want war, you must personally lead
your men to-morrow. We will not murder

women and children, but we will fight the
soldiers when they come." They then left
the council and hastened to warn my
brother-in-law, Faribault, and others who
were in danger.

Little Crow declared he would be seen in
the front of every battle, and it is true that
he was foremost in all the succeeding blood-
shed, urging his warriors to spare none. He
ordered his war leader, Many Hail, to fire
the first shot, killing the trader James
Lynd, in the door of his store.

After a year of fighting in which he had
met with defeat, the discredited chief retreated to Fort Garry, now Winnipeg,
Manitoba, where, together with Standing
Buffalo, he undertook secret negotiations
with his old friends the Indian traders.
There was now a price upon his head, but
he planned to·reach St. Paul undetected
and there surrender himself to his friends,
who he hoped would protect him in return
for past favors. It is true that he had
helped them to secure perhaps the finest

country held by any Indian nation for a
mere song.

He left Canada with a few trusted friends,
including his youngest and favorite son.
When within two or three days' journey
of St. Paul, he told the others to return,
keeping with him only his son, Wowinape,
who was but fifteen years of age. He meant
to steal into the city by night and go
straight to Governor Ramsey, who was his
personal friend. He was very hungry and
was obliged to keep to the shelter of the
deep woods. The next morning, as he was
picking and eating wild raspberries, he was
seen by a wood-chopper named Lamson.
The man did not know who he was. He only
knew that he was an Indian, and that was
enough for him, so he lifted his rifle to his
shoulder and fired, then ran at his best pace.
The brilliant but misguided chief, who had
made that part of the country unsafe for
any white man to live in, sank to the ground
and died without a struggle. The boy took
his father's gun and made some effort to

find the assassin, but as he did not even know in which direction to look for him, he soon gave up the attempt and went back to his friends.

Meanwhile Lamson reached home breathless and made his report. The body of the chief was found and identified, in part by the twice broken arm, and this arm and his scalp may be seen to-day in the collection of the Minnesota Historical Society.

TAMAHAY

THERE was once a Sioux brave who declared that he would die young, yet not by his own hand. Tamahay was of heroic proportions, herculean in strength, a superb runner; in fact, he had all the physical qualities of an athlete or a typical Indian. In his scanty dress, he was beautiful as an antique statue in living bronze. When a mere youth, seventeen years of age, he met with an accident which determined his career. It was the loss of an eye, a fatal injury to the sensitive and high-spirited Indian. He announced his purpose in these words :

"The 'Great Mystery' has decreed that I must be disgraced. There will be no pleasure for me now, and I shall be ridiculed even by my enemies. It will be well for me to enter soon into Paradise, for I shall

56

be happy in spending my youth there. But I will sell my life dearly. Hereafter my name shall be spoken in the traditions of our race." With this speech Tamahay began his career.

He now sought glory and defied danger with even more than the ordinary Indian recklessness. He accepted a personal friend, which was a custom among the Sioux, where each man chose a companion for life and death. The tie was stronger than one of blood relationship, a friendship sealed by solemn vow and covenant. Tamahay's intimate was fortunately almost his equal in physical powers, and the pair became the terror of neighboring tribes, with whom the Dakotas were continually at war. They made frequent raids upon their enemies and were usually successful, although not without thrilling experiences and almost miraculous escapes.

Upon one of these occasions the two friends went north into the country of the Ojibways. After many days' journey, they discovered a small village of the foe. The wicked Tamahay proposed to his associate that they should arrange their toilets after the fashion of the Ojibways, and go among them; "and perhaps," he added, "we will indulge in a little flirtation with their pretty maids, and when we have had enough of the fun we can take the scalp of a brave or two and retreat!" His friend construed his daring proposition to be a test of courage, which it would not become him, as a brave, to decline; therefore he assented with a show of cheerfulness.

The handsome strangers were well received by the Ojibway girls, but their perilous amusement was brought to an untimely close. A young maiden prematurely discovered their true characters, and her cry of alarm brought instantly to her side a jealous youth, who had been watching them from his place of concealment. With him Tamahay had a single-handed contest, and before a general alarm was given he had dispatched the foe and fled with his scalp.

The unfortunate brave had been a favorite and a leader among the tribe; therefore the maddened Ojibways were soon in hot pursuit. The Sioux braves were fine runners, yet they were finally driven out upon the peninsula of a lake. As they became separated in their retreat, Tamahay shouted, "I'll meet you at the mouth of the St. Croix River, or in the spirit land!" Both managed to swim the lake, and so made good their escape.

The exploits of this man were not all of a warlike nature. He was a great traveler and an expert scout, and he had some wonderful experiences with wild animals. He was once sent, with his intimate friend, on a scout for game. They were on ponies.

They located a herd of buffaloes, and on their return to the camp espied a lonely buffalo. Tamahay suggested that they should chase it in order to take some fresh meat, as the law of the tribe allowed in the case of a single animal. His pony stumbled and threw him, after they had wounded the bison, and the latter attacked the dismounted man viciously. But he, as usual, was on the alert. He "took the bull by the horns", as the saying is, and cleverly straddled him on the neck. The buffalo had no means of harming his enemy, but pawed the earth and struggled until his strength was exhausted, when the Indian used his knife on the animal's throat. On account of this feat he received the name "Held-the-Bull-by-the-Horns."

The origin of his name "Tamahay" is related as follows. When he was a young man he accompanied the chief Wabashaw to Mackinaw, Michigan, together with some other warriors. He was out with his friend one day, viewing the wonderful sights in the "white man's country", when they came upon a sow with her numerous pink little progeny. He was greatly amused and picked up one of the young pigs, but as soon as it squealed the mother ran furiously after them. He kept the pig and fled with it, still laughing; but his friend was soon com-

pelled to run up the conveniently inclined
trunk of a fallen tree, while our hero reached
the shore of a lake near by, and plunged into
the water. He swam and dived as long as
he could, but the beast continued to threaten
him with her sharp teeth, till, almost exhausted, he swam again to shore, where his
friend came up and dispatched the vicious
animal with a club. On account of this
watery adventure he was at once called
Tamahay, meaning Pike. He earned many
other names, but preferred this one, because
it was the name borne by a great friend
of his, Lieutenant Pike, the first officer
of the United States Army who came to
Minnesota for the purpose of exploring the
sources of the Mississippi River and of
making peace with the natives. Tamahay
assisted this officer in obtaining land from
the Sioux upon which to build Fort Snelling.
He appears in history under the name of
"Tahamie" or the "One-Eyed Sioux."

Always ready to brave danger and unpopularity, Tamahay was the only Sioux who

sided with the United States in her struggle
with Great Britain in 1812. For having
espoused the cause of the Americans, he
was ill-treated by the British officers and
free traders, who for a long time controlled
the northwest, even after peace had been
effected between the two nations. At one
time he was confined in a fort called McKay,
where now stands the town of Prairie du
Chien, Wisconsin. He had just returned
from St. Louis, and was suspected of exciting
his people to rebel against British subjects.
His life was even threatened, but to this
Tamahay merely replied that he was ready
to die. A few months later, this fort was
restored to the United States, and upon
leaving it the British set the buildings on
fire, though the United States flag floated
above them. Some Indians who were present shouted to Tamahay, "Your friends',
the Americans', fort is on fire!" He responded with a war whoop, rushed into the
blazing fort, and brought out the flag. For
this brave act he was rewarded with a

present of a flag and medal. He was never tired of displaying this medal and his recommendation papers, and even preserved to the end of his life an old colonial stovepipe hat, which he wore upon state occasions.

The Sioux long referred to the president of the United States as "Tamahay's father."

The following story is told of him in his later days. He attempted one day to cross the first bridge over the Mississippi River, but was not recognized by the sentinel, who would not allow him to pass until he paid the toll. Tamahay, who was a privileged character, explained as best he could, with gestures and broken English, that he was always permitted to pass free; but as the sentinel still refused, and even threatened him with his bayonet, the old Indian silently seized the musket, threw it down into the waters of the Mississippi and went home. Later in the day a company of soldiers appeared in the Indian village, and escorted our hero to a sort of court-martial at the

fort. When he was questioned by the
Colonel, he simply replied : "If you were
threatened by any one with a weapon, you
would, in self-defense, either disable the man
or get rid of the weapon. I did the latter,
thinking that you would need the man more
than the gun."

Finally the officer said to them, "I see
you are both partly wrong. Some one must
be responsible for the loss of the gun ; therefore, you two will wrestle, and the man who
is downed must dive for the weapon to the
bottom of the river."

Scarcely was this speech ended when
Tamahay was upon the soldier, who was
surprised both by the order and by the
unexpected readiness of the wily old Indian,
so that he was not prepared, and the Sioux
had the vantage hold. In a moment the
bluecoat was down, amid shouts and peals
of laughter from his comrades. Having
thrown his man, the other turned and went
home without a word.

Sad to say, he acquired a great appetite

for "minne-wakan", or "mysterious water ",
as the Sioux call it, which proved a source
of trouble to him in his old age. It is told
of him that he was treated one winter's day
to a drink of whisky in a trader's store.
He afterwards went home; but even the
severe blizzard which soon arose did not
prevent him from returning in the night to
the friendly trader. He awoke that worthy
from sleep about twelve o'clock by singing
his death dirge upon the roof of the log
cabin. In another moment he had jumped
down the mud chimney, and into the blazing
embers of a fire. The trader had to pour
out to him some whisky in a tin pail, after
which he begged the old man to "be good
and go home." On the eve of the so-called
"Minnesota Massacre" by the Sioux in 1862,
Tamahay, although he was then very old
and had almost lost the use of his remaining
eye, made a famous speech at the meeting
of the conspirators. These are some of his
words, as reported to me by persons who
were present.

"What! What! is this Little Crow?
Is that Little Six? You, too, White Dog,
are you here? I cannot see well now, but
I can see with my mind's eye the stream of
blood you are about to pour upon the bosom
of this mother of ours" (meaning the
earth). "I stand before you on three legs,
but the third leg has brought me wisdom"
[referring to the staff with which he supported himself]. "I have traveled much,
I have visited among the people whom you
think to defy. This means the total surrender of our beautiful land, the land of
a thousand lakes and streams. Methinks
you are about to commit an act like that of
the porcupine, who climbs a tree, balances
himself upon a springy bough, and then
gnaws off the very bough upon which he is
sitting; hence, when it gives way, he falls
upon the sharp rocks below. Behold the
great Pontiac, whose grave I saw near St.
Louis; he was murdered while an exile from
his country! Think of the brave Black
Hawk! Methinks his spirit is still wailing

through Winconsin and Illinois for his lost people! I do not say you have no cause to complain, but to resist is self-destruction. I am done."

It is supposed that this speech was his last, and it was made, though vainly, in defense of the Americans whom he had loved. He died at Fort Pierre, South Dakota, in 1864. His people say that he died a natural death, of old age. And yet his exploits are not forgotten. Thus lived and departed a most active and fearless Sioux, Tamahay, who desired to die young!

GALL

CHIEF GALL was one of the most aggressive leaders of the Sioux nation in their last stand for freedom.

The westward pressure of civilization during the past three centuries has been tremendous. When our hemisphere was "discovered", it had been inhabited by the natives for untold ages, but it was held undiscovered because the original owners did not chart or advertise it. Yet some of them at least had developed ideals of life which included *real* liberty and equality to all men, and they did not recognize individual ownership in land or other property beyond actual necessity. It was a soul development leading to essential manhood. Under this system they brought forth some striking characters.

Gall was considered by both Indians and

whites to be a most impressive type of physical manhood. From his picture you can judge of this for yourself.

Let us follow his trail. He was no tenderfoot. He never asked a soft place for himself. He always played the game according to the rules and to a finish. To be sure, like every other man, he made some mistakes, but he was an Indian and never acted the coward.

The earliest stories told of his life and doings indicate the spirit of the man in that of the boy.

When he was only about three years old, the Blackfoot band of Sioux were on their usual roving hunt, following the buffalo while living their natural happy life upon the wonderful wide prairies of the Dakotas.

It was the way of every Sioux mother to adjust her household effects on such dogs and pack ponies as she could muster from day to day, often lending one or two to accommodate some other woman whose horse or dog had died, or perhaps had been among those stampeded and carried away by a raiding band of Crow warriors. On this particular occasion, the mother of our young Sioux brave, Matohinshda, or Bear-Shedding-His-Hair (Gall's childhood name), intrusted her boy to an old Eskimo pack dog, experienced and reliable, except perhaps when unduly excited or very thirsty.

On the day of removing camp the caravan made its morning march up the Powder River. Upon the wide table-land the women were busily digging teepsinna (an edible sweetish root, much used by them) as the moving village slowly progressed. As usual at such times, the trail was wide. An old jack rabbit had waited too long in hiding. Now, finding himself almost surrounded by the mighty plains people, he sprang up suddenly, his feathery ears conspicuously erect, a dangerous challenge to the dogs and the people.

A whoop went up. Every dog accepted the challenge. Forgotten were the bundles, the kits, even the babies they were drawing or carrying. The chase was on, and the screams of the women reëchoed from the opposite cliffs of the Powder, mingled with the yelps of dogs and the neighing of horses. The hand of every man was against the daring warrior, the lone Jack, and the confusion was great.

When the fleeing one cleared the mass of his enemies, he emerged with a swiftness that commanded respect and gave promise of a determined chase. Behind him, his pursuers stretched out in a thin line, first the speedy, unburdened dogs and then the travois dogs headed by the old Eskimo with his precious freight. The youthful Gall was in a travois, a basket mounted on trailing poles and harnessed to the sides of the animal.

"Hey! hey! they are gaining on him!" a warrior shouted. At this juncture two of the canines had almost nabbed their furry prey by the back. But he was too cunning for them. He dropped instantly and sent both dogs over his head, rolling and spinning, then made another flight at right angles to the first. This gave the Eskimo a chance to cut the triangle. He gained fifty yards, but being heavily handicapped, two unladen dogs passed him. The same trick was repeated by the Jack, and this time he saved himself from instant death by a double loop and was now running directly toward the crowd, followed by a dozen or more dogs. He was losing speed, but likewise his pursuers were dropping off steadily. Only the sturdy Eskimo dog held to his even gait, and behind him in the frail travois leaned forward the little Matohinshda, nude save a breech clout, his left hand holding fast the convenient tail of his dog, the right grasping firmly one of the poles of the travois. His black eyes were bulging almost out of their sockets; his long hair flowed out behind like a stream of dark water.

The Jack now ran directly toward the howling spectators, but his marvelous speed and alertness were on the wane; while on

the other hand his foremost pursuer, who
had taken part in hundreds of similar events,
had every confidence in his own endurance.
Each leap brought him nearer, fiercer and
more determined. The last effort of the
Jack was to lose himself in the crowd, like
a fish in muddy water; but the big dog made
the one needed leap with unerring aim and
his teeth flashed as he caught the rabbit in
viselike jaws and held him limp in air, a
victor!

The people rushed up to him as he laid
the victim down, and foremost among them
was the frantic mother of Matohinshda, or
Gall. "Michinkshe! michinkshe!" (My
son! my son!) she screamed as she drew
near. The boy seemed to be none the
worse for his experience. "Mother!" he
cried, "my dog is brave: he got the rabbit!"
She snatched him off the travois, but he
struggled out of her arms to look upon his
dog lovingly and admiringly. Old men and
boys crowded about the hero of the day, the
dog, and the thoughtful grandmother of

Matohinshda unharnessed him and poured some water from a parfleche water bag into a basin. "Here, my grandson, give your friend something to drink."

"How, hechetu," pronounced an old warrior no longer in active service. "This may be only an accident, an ordinary affair; but such things sometimes indicate a career. The boy has had a wonderful ride. I prophesy that he will one day hold the attention of all the people with his doings."

This is the first remembered story of the famous chief, but other boyish exploits foretold the man he was destined to be. He fought many sham battles, some successful and others not; but he was always a fierce fighter and a good loser.

Once he was engaged in a battle with snowballs. There were probably nearly a hundred boys on each side, and the rule was that every fair hit made the receiver officially dead. He must not participate further, but must remain just where he was struck.

Gall's side was fast losing, and the battle was growing hotter every minute when the youthful warrior worked toward an old water hole and took up his position there. His side was soon annihilated and there were eleven men left to fight him. He was pressed close in the wash-out, and as he dodged under cover before a volley of snowballs, there suddenly emerged in his stead a huge gray wolf. His opponents fled in every direction in superstitious terror, for they thought he had been transformed into the animal. To their astonishment he came out on the farther side and ran to the line of safety, a winner!

It happened that the wolf's den had been partly covered with snow so that no one had noticed it until the yells of the boys aroused the inmate, and he beat a hasty retreat. The boys always looked upon this incident as an omen.

Gall had an amiable disposition but was quick to resent insult or injustice. This sometimes involved him in difficulties, but he seldom fought without good cause and was popular with his associates. One of his characteristics was his ability to organize, and this was a large factor in his leadership when he became a man. He was tried in many ways, and never was known to hesitate when it was a question of physical courage and endurance. He entered the public service early in life, but not until he had proved himself competent and passed all tests.

When a mere boy, he was once scouting for game in midwinter, far from camp, and was overtaken by a three days' blizzard. He was forced to abandon his horse and lie under the snow for that length of time. He afterward said he was not particularly hungry; it was thirst and stiffness from which he suffered most. One reason the Indian so loved his horse or dog was that at such times the animal would stay by him like a brother. On this occasion Gall's pony was not more than a stone's throw away when the storm subsided and the sun shone. There was a herd of buffalo in plain sight, and the young hunter was not long in procuring a meal.

This chief's contemporaries still recall his wrestling match with the equally powerful Cheyenne boy, Roman Nose, who afterward became a chief well known to American history. It was a custom of the northwestern Indians, when two friendly tribes camped together, to establish the physical and athletic supremacy of the youth of the respective camps.

The "Che-hoo-hoo" is a wrestling game in which there may be any number on a side, but the numbers are equal. All the boys of each camp are called together by a leader chosen for the purpose and draw themselves up in line of battle; then each at a given signal attacks his opponent.

In this memorable contest, Matohinshda, or Gall, was placed opposite Roman Nose. The whole people turned out as spectators of the struggle, and the battlefield was a plateau between the two camps, in the midst of picturesque Bad Lands. There were many athletic youths present, but these two were really the Apollos of the two tribes.

In this kind of sport it is not allowed to strike with the hand, nor catch around the neck, nor kick, nor pull by the hair. One may break away and run a few yards to get a fresh start, or clinch, or catch as catch can. When a boy is thrown and held to the ground, he is counted out. If a boy has met his superior, he may drop to the ground to escape rough handling, but it is very seldom one gives up without a full trial of strength.

It seemed almost like a real battle, so great was the enthusiasm, as the shouts of sympathizers on both sides went up in a mighty chorus. At last all were either conquerors or subdued except Gall and Roman Nose. The pair seemed equally matched. Both were stripped to the breech clout, now tugging like two young buffalo or elk in mating time, again writhing and

twisting like serpents. At times they fought
like two wild stallions, straining every mus-
cle of arms, legs, and back in the struggle.
Every now and then one was lifted off his
feet for a moment, but came down planted
like a tree, and after swaying to and fro soon
became rigid again.

All eyes were upon the champions.
Finally, either by trick or main force, Gall
laid the other sprawling upon the ground
and held him fast for a minute, then
released him and stood erect, panting, a
master youth. Shout after shout went up
on the Sioux side of the camp. The mother
of Roman Nose came forward and threw a
superbly worked buffalo robe over Gall,
whose mother returned the compliment by
covering the young Cheyenne with a handsome blanket.

Undoubtedly these early contests had
their influence upon our hero's career. It
was his habit to appear most opportunely
in a crisis, and in a striking and dramatic
manner to take command of the situation.

The best known example of this is his
entrance on the scene of confusion when
Reno surprised the Sioux on the Little Big
Horn.   Many of the excitable youths, almost unarmed, rushed madly and blindly
to meet the intruder, and the scene might
have unnerved even an experienced warrior.
It was Gall, with not a garment upon his
superb body, who on his black charger
dashed ahead of the boys and faced them.
He stopped them on the dry creek, while
the bullets of Reno's men whistled about
their ears.

"Hold hard, men! Steady, we are not
ready yet! Wait for more guns, more
horses, and the day is yours!"

They obeyed, and in a few minutes the
signal to charge was given, and Reno retreated pell mell before the onset of the
Sioux.

Sitting Bull had confidence in his men
so long as Gall planned and directed the
attack, whether against United States soldiers or the warriors of another tribe.   He

GALL

was a strategist, and able in a twinkling to note and seize upon an advantage. He was really the mainstay of Sitting Bull's effective last stand. He consistently upheld his people's right to their buffalo plains and believed that they should hold the government strictly to its agreements with them. When the treaty of 1868 was disregarded, he agreed with Sitting Bull in defending the last of their once vast domain, and after the Custer battle entered Canada with his chief. They hoped to bring their lost cause before the English government and were much disappointed when they were asked to return to the United States.

Gall finally reported at Fort Peck, Montana, in 1881, and brought half of the Hunkpapa band with him, whereupon he was soon followed by Sitting Bull himself. Although they had been promised by the United States commission who went to Canada to treat with them that they would not be punished if they returned, no sooner had Gall come down than a part of his people were attacked, and in the spring they were all brought to Fort Randall and held as military prisoners. From this point they were returned to Standing Rock agency.

When "Buffalo Bill" successfully launched his first show, he made every effort to secure both Sitting Bull and Gall for his leading attractions. The military was in complete accord with him in this, for they still had grave suspicions of these two leaders. While Sitting Bull reluctantly agreed, Gall haughtily said: "I am not an animal to be exhibited before the crowd," and retired to his teepee. His spirit was much worn, and he lost strength from that time on. That superb manhood dwindled, and in a few years he died. He was a real hero of a free and natural people, a type that is never to be seen again.

CRAZY HORSE

CRAZY HORSE was born on the Republican River about 1845. He was killed at Fort Robinson, Nebraska, in 1877, so that he lived barely thirty-three years.

He was an uncommonly handsome man. While not the equal of Gall in magnificence and imposing stature, he was physically perfect, an Apollo in symmetry. Furthermore he was a true type of Indian refinement and grace. He was modest and courteous as Chief Joseph; the difference is that he was a born warrior, while Joseph was not. However, he was a gentle warrior, a true brave, who stood for the highest ideal of the Sioux. Notwithstanding all that biased historians have said of him, it is only fair to judge a man by the estimate of his own people rather than that of his enemies.

The boyhood of Crazy Horse was passed in the days when the western Sioux saw a white man but seldom, and then it was usually a trader or a soldier. He was carefully brought up according to the tribal customs. At that period the Sioux prided themselves on the training and development of their sons and daughters, and not a step in that development was overlooked as an excuse to bring the child before the public by giving a feast in its honor. At such times the parents often gave so generously to the needy that they almost impoverished themselves, thus setting an example to the child of self-denial for the general good. His first step alone, the first word spoken, first game killed, the attainment of manhood or womanhood, each was the occasion of a feast and dance in his honor, at which the poor always benefited to the full extent of the parents' ability.

Big-heartedness, generosity, courage, and self-denial are the qualifications of a public servant, and the average Indian was keen to follow this ideal. As every one knows, these characteristic traits become a weakness when he enters a life founded upon commerce and gain. Under such conditions the life of Crazy Horse began. His mother, like other mothers, tender and watchful of her boy, would never once place an obstacle in the way of his father's severe physical training. They laid the spiritual and patriotic foundations of his education in such a way that he early became conscious of the demands of public service.

He was perhaps four or five years old when the band was snowed in one severe winter. They were very short of food, but his father was a tireless hunter. The buffalo, their main dependence, were not to be found, but he was out in the storm and cold every day and finally brought in two antelopes. The little boy got on his pet pony and rode through the camp, telling the old folks to come to his mother's teepee for meat. It turned out that neither his father nor mother had authorized him to do this. Before they knew it, old men and women were lined up before the teepee home, ready to receive the meat, in answer to his invitation. As a result, the mother had to distribute nearly all of it, keeping only enough for two meals.

On the following day the child asked for food. His mother told him that the old folks had taken it all, and added: "Remember, my son, they went home singing praises in your name, not my name or your father's. You must be brave. You must live up to your reputation."

Crazy Horse loved horses, and his father gave him a pony of his own when he was very young. He became a fine horseman and accompanied his father on buffalo hunts, holding the pack horses while the men chased the buffalo and thus gradually learning the art. In those days the Sioux had but few guns, and the hunting was mostly done with bow and arrows.

Another story told of his boyhood is that when he was about twelve he went to look for the ponies with his little brother, whom he loved much, and took a great deal of pains to teach what he had already learned. They came to some wild cherry trees full of ripe fruit, and while they were enjoying it, the brothers were startled by the growl and sudden rush of a bear. Young Crazy Horse pushed his brother up into the nearest tree and himself sprang upon the back of one of the horses, which was frightened and ran some distance before he could control him. As soon as he could, however, he turned him about and came back, yelling and swinging his lariat over his head. The bear at first showed fight but finally turned and ran. The old man who told me this story added that young as he was, he had some power, so that even a grizzly did not care to tackle him. I believe it is a fact that a silver-tip will dare anything except a bell or a lasso line, so that accidentally the boy had hit upon the very thing which would drive him off.

It was usual for Sioux boys of his day to wait in the field after a buffalo hunt until sundown, when the young calves would come out in the open, hungrily seeking their mothers. Then these wild children would enjoy a mimic hunt, and lasso the calves or drive them into camp. Crazy Horse was found to be a determined little fellow, and it was settled one day among the larger boys that they would "stump" him to ride a good-sized bull calf. He rode the calf, and stayed on its back while it ran bawling over the hills, followed by the other boys on their ponies, until his strange mount stood trembling and exhausted.

At the age of sixteen he joined a war party against the Gros Ventres. He was well in the front of the charge, and at once established his bravery by following closely

one of the foremost Sioux warriors, by the
name of Hump, drawing the enemy's fire
and circling around their advance guard.
Suddenly Hump's horse was shot from
under him, and there was a rush of warriors
to kill or capture him while down. But
amidst a shower of arrows the youth leaped
from his pony, helped his friend into his
own saddle, sprang up behind him, and
carried him off in safety, although they
were hotly pursued by the enemy. Thus
he associated himself in his maiden battle
with the wizard of Indian warfare, and
Hump, who was then at the height of his
own career, pronounced Crazy Horse the
coming warrior of the Teton Sioux.

At this period of his life, as was customary with the best young men, he spent
much time in prayer and solitude. Just
what happened in these days of his fasting
in the wilderness and upon the crown of
bald buttes, no one will ever know; for
these things may only be known when one
has lived through the battles of life to an

honored old age. He was much sought after by his youthful associates, but was noticeably reserved and modest; yet in the moment of danger he at once rose above them all — a natural leader! Crazy Horse was a typical Sioux brave, and from the point of view of our race an ideal hero, living at the height of the epical progress of the American Indian and maintaining in his own character all that was most subtle and ennobling of their spiritual life, and that has since been lost in the contact with a material civilization.

He loved Hump, that peerless warrior, and the two became close friends, in spite of the difference in age. Men called them "the grizzly and his cub." Again and again the pair saved the day for the Sioux in a skirmish with some neighboring tribe. But one day they undertook a losing battle against the Snakes. The Sioux were in full retreat and were fast being overwhelmed by superior numbers. The old warrior fell in a last desperate charge;

but Crazy Horse and his younger brother,
though dismounted, killed two of the enemy
and thus made good their retreat.

It was observed of him that when he
pursued the enemy into their stronghold,
as he was wont to do, he often refrained
from killing, and simply struck them with
a switch, showing that he did not fear
their weapons nor care to waste his upon
them. In attempting this very feat, he
lost this only brother of his, who emulated
him closely. A party of young warriors,
led by Crazy Horse, had dashed upon a
frontier post, killed one of the sentinels,
stampeded the horses, and pursued the
herder to the very gate of the stockade,
thus drawing upon themselves the fire of
the garrison. The leader escaped without
a scratch, but his young brother was
brought down from his horse and killed.

While he was still under twenty, there
was a great winter buffalo hunt, and he
came back with ten buffaloes' tongues
which he sent to the council lodge for the

councilors' feast. He had in one winter day killed ten buffalo cows with his bow and arrows, and the unsuccessful hunters or those who had no swift ponies were made happy by his generosity. When the hunters returned, these came chanting songs of thanks. He knew that his father was an expert hunter and had a good horse, so he took no meat home, putting in practice the spirit of his early teaching.

He attained his majority at the crisis of the difficulties between the United States and the Sioux. Even before that time, Crazy Horse had already proved his worth to his people in Indian warfare. He had risked his life again and again, and in some instances it was considered almost a miracle that he had saved others as well as himself. He was no orator nor was he the son of a chief. His success and influence was purely a matter of personality. He had never fought the whites up to this time, and indeed no "coup" was counted for killing or scalping a white man.

Young Crazy Horse was twenty-one years old when all the Teton Sioux chiefs (the western or plains dwellers) met in council to determine upon their future policy toward the invader. Their former agreements had been by individual bands, each for itself, and every one was friendly. They reasoned that the country was wide, and that the white traders should be made welcome. Up to this time they had anticipated no conflict. They had permitted the Oregon Trail, but now to their astonishment forts were built and garrisoned in their territory.

Most of the chiefs advocated a strong resistance. There were a few influential men who desired still to live in peace, and who were willing to make another treaty. Among these were White Bull, Two Kettle, Four Bears, and Swift Bear. Even Spotted Tail, afterward the great peace chief, was at this time with the majority, who decided in the year 1866 to defend their rights and territory by force. Attacks were to be made upon the forts within their country and on every trespasser on the same.

Crazy Horse took no part in the discussion, but he and all the young warriors were in accord with the decision of the council. Although so young, he was already a leader among them. Other prominent young braves were Sword (brother of the man of that name who was long captain of police at Pine Ridge), the younger Hump, Charging Bear, Spotted Elk, Crow King, No Water, Big Road, He Dog, the nephew of Red Cloud, and Touch-the-Cloud, intimate friend of Crazy Horse.

The attack on Fort Phil Kearny was the first fruits of the new policy, and here Crazy Horse was chosen to lead the attack on the woodchoppers, designed to draw the soldiers out of the fort, while an army of six hundred lay in wait for them. The success of this stratagem was further enhanced by his masterful handling of his men. From this time on a general war

was inaugurated; Sitting Bull looked to
him as a principal war leader, and even the
Cheyenne chiefs, allies of the Sioux, practically acknowledged his leadership. Yet
during the following ten years of defensive
war he was never known to make a speech,
though his teepee was the rendezvous of
the young men. He was depended upon
to put into action the decisions of the
council, and was frequently consulted by
the older chiefs.

Like Osceola, he rose suddenly; like
Tecumseh he was always impatient for
battle; like Pontiac, he fought on while
his allies were suing for peace, and like
Grant, the silent soldier, he was a man of
deeds and not of words. He won from
Custer and Fetterman and Crook. He
won every battle that he undertook, with
the exception of one or two occasions when
he was surprised in the midst of his women
and children, and even then he managed
to extricate himself in safety from a difficult position.

Early in the year 1876, his runners
brought word from Sitting Bull that all
the roving bands would converge upon the
upper Tongue River in Montana for summer feasts and conferences. There was
conflicting news from the reservation. It
was rumored that the army would fight
the Sioux to a finish; again, it was said
that another commission would be sent
out to treat with them.

The Indians came together early in
June, and formed a series of encampments
stretching out from three to four miles,
each band keeping separate camp. On
June 17, scouts came in and reported the
advance of a large body of troops under
General Crook. The council sent Crazy
Horse with seven hundred men to meet
and attack him. These were nearly all
young men, many of them under twenty,
the flower of the hostile Sioux. They set
out at night so as to steal a march upon
the enemy, but within three or four miles
of his camp they came unexpectedly upon

some of his Crow scouts. There was a hurried exchange of shots; the Crows fled back to Crook's camp, pursued by the Sioux. The soldiers had their warning, and it was impossible to enter the well-protected camp. Again and again Crazy Horse charged with his bravest men, in the attempt to bring the troops into the open, but he succeeded only in drawing their fire. Toward afternoon he withdrew, and returned to camp disappointed. His scouts remained to watch Crook's movements, and later brought word that he had retreated to Goose Creek and seemed to have no further disposition to disturb the Sioux. It is well known to us that it is Crook rather than Reno who is to be blamed for cowardice in connection with Custer's fate. The latter had no chance to do anything, he was lucky to save himself; but if Crook had kept on his way, as ordered, to meet Terry, with his one thousand regulars and two hundred Crow and Shoshone scouts, he would in-

evitably have intercepted Custer in his
advance and saved the day for him, and
war with the Sioux would have ended
right there. Instead of this, he fell back
upon Fort Meade, eating his horses on the
way, in a country swarming with game,
for fear of Crazy Horse and his braves!

The Indians now crossed the divide
between the Tongue and the Little Big
Horn, where they felt safe from immediate
pursuit. Here, with all their precautions,
they were caught unawares by General
Custer, in the midst of their midday games
and festivities, while many were out upon
the daily hunt.

On this twenty-fifth of June, 1876, the
great camp was scattered for three miles
or more along the level river bottom, back
of the thin line of cottonwoods — five
circular rows of teepees, ranging from half
a mile to a mile and a half in circumference.
Here and there stood out a large, white,
solitary teepee; these were the lodges or
"clubs" of the young men. Crazy Horse

was a member of the "Strong Hearts" and the "Tokala" or Fox lodge. He was watching a game of ring-toss when the warning came from the southern end of the camp of the approach of troops.

The Sioux and the Cheyennes were "minute men", and although taken by surprise, they instantly responded. Meanwhile, the women and children were thrown into confusion. Dogs were howling, ponies running hither and thither, pursued by their owners, while many of the old men were singing their lodge songs to encourage the warriors, or praising the "strong heart" of Crazy Horse.

That leader had quickly saddled his favorite war pony and was starting with his young men for the south end of the camp, when a fresh alarm came from the opposite direction, and looking up, he saw Custer's force upon the top of the bluff directly across the river. As quick as a flash, he took in the situation — the enemy had planned to attack the camp at both ends at once; and knowing that Custer could not ford the river at that point, he instantly led his men northward to the ford to cut him off. The Cheyennes followed closely. Custer must have seen that wonderful dash up the sage-bush plain, and one wonders whether he realized its meaning. In a very few minutes, this wild general of the plains had outwitted one of the most brilliant leaders of the Civil War and ended at once his military career and his life.

In this dashing charge, Crazy Horse snatched his most famous victory out of what seemed frightful peril, for the Sioux could not know how many were behind Custer. He was caught in his own trap. To the soldiers it must have seemed as if the Indians rose up from the earth to overwhelm them. They closed in from three sides and fought until not a white man was left alive. Then they went down to Reno's stand and found him so well intrenched in a deep gully that it was impossible to dislodge him. Gall and his men held him there until the approach of General Terry compelled the Sioux to break camp and scatter in different directions.

While Sitting Bull was pursued into Canada, Crazy Horse and the Cheyennes wandered about, comparatively undisturbed, during the rest of that year, until in the winter the army surprised the Cheyennes, but did not do them much harm, possibly because they knew that Crazy Horse was not far off. His name was held in wholesome respect. From time to time, delegations of friendly Indians were sent to him, to urge him to come in to the reservation, promising a full hearing and fair treatment.

For some time he held out, but the rapid disappearance of the buffalo, their only means of support, probably weighed with him more than any other influence. In July, 1877, he was finally prevailed upon to come in to Fort Robinson, Nebraska, with several thousand Indians, most of them Ogallala and Minneconwoju Sioux, on the distinct understanding that the government would hear and adjust their grievances.

At this juncture General Crook proclaimed Spotted Tail, who had rendered much valuable service to the army, head chief of the Sioux, which was resented by many. The attention paid Crazy Horse was offensive to Spotted Tail and the Indian scouts, who planned a conspiracy against him. They reported to General Crook that the young chief would murder him at the next council, and stampede the Sioux into another war. He was urged not to attend the council and did not, but sent another officer to represent him. Meanwhile the friends of Crazy Horse discovered the plot and told him of it. His reply was, "Only cowards are murderers."

His wife was critically ill at the time, and he decided to take her to her parents at Spotted Tail agency, whereupon his

enemies circulated the story that he had
fled, and a party of scouts was sent after
him. They overtook him riding with his
wife and one other but did not undertake
to arrest him, and after he had left the
sick woman with her people he went to
call on Captain Lea, the agent for the
Brulés, accompanied by all the warriors of
the Minneconwoju band. This volunteer
escort made an imposing appearance on
horseback, shouting and singing, and in
the words of Captain Lea himself and the
missionary, the Reverend Mr. Cleveland,
the situation was extremely critical. Indeed, the scouts who had followed Crazy
Horse from Red Cloud agency were advised not to show themselves, as some of
the warriors had urged that they be taken
out and horsewhipped publicly.

Under these circumstances Crazy Horse
again showed his masterful spirit by holding these young men in check. He said
to them in his quiet way: "It is well to
be brave in the field of battle; it is cow-

ardly to display bravery against one's own
tribesmen. These scouts have been compelled to do what they did; they are no
better than servants of the white officers.
I came here on a peaceful errand."

The captain urged him to report at
army headquarters to explain himself and
correct false rumors, and on his giving
consent, furnished him with a wagon and
escort. It has been said that he went back
under arrest, but this is untrue. Indians
have boasted that they had a hand in
bringing him in, but their stories are without foundation. He went of his own accord, either suspecting no treachery or
determined to defy it.

When he reached the military camp,
Little Big Man walked arm-in-arm with
him, and his cousin and friend, Touch-
the-Cloud, was just in advance. After
they passed the sentinel, an officer approached them and walked on his other
side. He was unarmed but for the knife
which is carried for ordinary uses by

women as well as men. Unsuspectingly he walked toward the guardhouse, when Touch-the-Cloud suddenly turned back exclaiming: "Cousin, they will put you in prison!"

"Another white man's trick! Let me go! Let me die fighting!" cried Crazy Horse. He stopped and tried to free himself and draw his knife, but both arms were held fast by Little Big Man and the officer. While he struggled thus, a soldier thrust him through with his bayonet from behind. The wound was mortal, and he died in the course of that night, his old father singing the death song over him and afterward carrying away the body, which they said must not be further polluted by the touch of a white man. They hid it somewhere in the Bad Lands, his resting place to this day.

Thus died one of the ablest and truest American Indians. His life was ideal; his record clean. He was never involved in any of the numerous massacres on the trail, but was a leader in practically every open fight. Such characters as those of Crazy Horse and Chief Joseph are not easily found among so-called civilized people. The reputation of great men is apt to be shadowed by questionable motives and policies, but here are two pure patriots, as worthy of honor as any who ever breathed God's air in the wide spaces of a new world.

SITTING BULL

IT is not easy to characterize Sitting Bull, of all Sioux chiefs most generally known to the American people. There are few to whom his name is not familiar, and still fewer who have learned to connect it with anything more than the conventional notion of a bloodthirsty savage. The man was an enigma at best. He was not impulsive, nor was he phlegmatic. He was most serious when he seemed to be jocose. He was gifted with the power of sarcasm, and few have used it more artfully than he.

His father was one of the best-known members of the Unkpapa band of Sioux. The manner of this man's death was characteristic. One day, when the Unkpapas were attacked by a large war party of Crows, he fell upon the enemy's war

107

leader with his knife. In a hand-to-hand combat of this sort, we count the victor as entitled to a war bonnet of trailing plumes. It means certain death to one or both. In this case, both men dealt a mortal stroke, and Jumping Buffalo, the father of Sitting Bull, fell from his saddle and died in a few minutes. The other died later from the effects of the wound.

Sitting Bull's boyhood must have been a happy one. It was long after the day of the dog-travaux, and his father owned many ponies of variegated colors. It was said of him in a joking way that his legs were bowed like the ribs of the ponies that he rode constantly from childhood· He had also a common nickname that was much to the point. It was "Hunkeshnee", which means "Slow", referring to his inability to run fast, or more probably to the fact that he seldom appeared on foot. In their boyish games he was wont to take the part of the "old man", but this does not mean that he was not active and brave.

It is told that after a buffalo hunt the
boys were enjoying a mimic hunt with the
calves that had been left behind. A large
calf turned viciously on Sitting Bull, whose
pony had thrown him, but the alert youth
got hold of both ears and struggled until
the calf was pushed back into a buffalo
wallow in a sitting posture. The boys
shouted: "He has subdued the buffalo
calf! He made it sit down!" And from
this incident was derived his familiar name
of Sitting Bull.

It is a mistake to suppose that Sitting
Bull, or any other Indian warrior, was of
a murderous disposition. It is true that
savage warfare had grown more and more
harsh and cruel since the coming of white
traders among them, bringing guns, knives,
and whisky. Yet it was still regarded
largely as a sort of game, undertaken in
order to develop the manly qualities of
their youth. It was the degree of risk
which brought honor, rather than the
number slain, and a brave must mourn

thirty days, with blackened face and loosened hair, for the enemy whose life he had taken. While the spoils of war were allowed, this did not extend to territorial aggrandizement, nor was there any wish to overthrow another nation and enslave its people. It was a point of honor in the old days to treat a captive with kindness. The common impression that the Indian is naturally cruel and revengeful is entirely opposed to his philosophy and training. The revengeful tendency of the Indian was aroused by the white man. It is not the natural Indian who is mean and tricky; not Massasoit but King Philip; not Attackullakulla but Weatherford; not Wabashaw but Little Crow; not Jumping Buffalo but Sitting Bull! These men lifted their hands against the white man, while their fathers held theirs out to him with gifts.

Remember that there were councils which gave their decisions in accordance with the highest ideal of human justice before there were any cities on this continent; before there were bridges to span the Mississippi; before this network of railroads was dreamed of! There were primitive communities upon the very spot where Chicago or New York City now stands, where men were as children, innocent of all the crimes now committed there daily and nightly. True morality is more easily maintained in connection with the simple life. You must accept the truth that you demoralize any race whom you have subjugated.

From this point of view we shall consider Sitting Bull's career. We say he is an untutored man : that is true so far as learning of a literary type is concerned; but he was not an untutored man when you view him from the standpoint of his nation. To be sure, he did not learn his lessons from books. This is second-hand information at best. All that he learned he verified for himself and put into daily practice. In personal appearance he was rather commonplace and made no immediate impression, but as he talked he seemed to take hold of his hearers more and more. He was bull-headed; quick to grasp a situation, and not readily induced to change his mind. He was not suspicious until he was forced to be so. All his meaner traits were inevitably developed by the events of his later career.

Sitting Bull's history has been written many times by newspaper men and army officers, but I find no account of him which is entirely correct. I met him personally in 1884, and since his death I have gone thoroughly into the details of his life with his relatives and contemporaries. It has often been said that he was a physical coward and not a warrior. Judge of this for yourselves from the deed which first gave him fame in his own tribe, when he was about twenty-eight years old.

In an attack upon a band of Crow Indians, one of the enemy took his stand, after the rest had fled, in a deep ditch from which it seemed impossible to dislodge him. The situation had already cost the lives of several warriors, but they could not let him go to repeat such a boast over the Sioux!

"Follow me!" said Sitting Bull, and charged. He raced his horse to the brim of the ditch and struck at the enemy with his coup-staff, thus compelling him to expose himself to the fire of the others while shooting his assailant. But the Crow merely poked his empty gun into his face and dodged back under cover. Then Sitting Bull stopped; he saw that no one had followed him, and he also perceived that the enemy had no more ammunition left. He rode deliberately up to the barrier and threw his loaded gun over it; then he went back to his party and told them what he thought of them.

"Now," said he, "I have armed him, for I will not see a brave man killed unarmed. I will strike him again with my coup-staff to count the first feather; who will count the second?"

Again he led the charge, and this time they all followed him. Sitting Bull was severely wounded by his own gun in the hands of the enemy, who was killed by those that came after him. This is a record that so far as I know was never made by any other warrior.

The second incident that made him well known was his taking of a boy captive in battle with the Assiniboines. He saved this boy's life and adopted him as his brother. Hóhay, as he was called, was devoted to Sitting Bull and helped much in later years to spread his fame. Sitting Bull was a born diplomat, a ready speaker, and in middle life he ceased to go upon the warpath, to become the councilor of his people. From this time on, this man represented him in all important battles, and upon every brave deed done was wont to exclaim aloud:

"I, Sitting Bull's boy, do this in his name!"

He had a nephew, now living, who re-

sembles him strongly, and who also represented him personally upon the field;
and so far as there is any remnant left of
his immediate band, they look upon this
man One Bull as their chief.

When Sitting Bull was a boy, there was
no thought of trouble with the whites.
He was acquainted with many of the early
traders, Picotte, Choteau, Primeau, Lar-
penteur, and others, and liked them, as
did most of his people in those days. All
the early records show this friendly atti-
tude of the Sioux, and the great fur
companies for a century and a half depended upon them for the bulk of their
trade. It was not until the middle of the
last century that they woke up all of a
sudden to the danger threatening their
very existence. Yet at that time many of
the old chiefs had been already depraved
by the whisky and other vices of the whites,
and in the vicinity of the forts and trading
posts at Sioux City, Saint Paul, and
Cheyenne, there was general demorali-

zation. The drunkards and hangers-on were ready to sell almost anything they had for the favor of the trader. The better and stronger element held aloof. They would not have anything of the white man except his hatchet, gun, and knife. They utterly refused to cede their lands; and as for the rest, they were willing to let him alone as long as he did not interfere with their life and customs, which was not long.

It was not, however, the Unkpapa band of Sioux, Sitting Bull's band, which first took up arms against the whites; and this was not because they had come less in contact with them, for they dwelt on the Missouri River, the natural highway of trade. As early as 1854, the Ogallalas and Brulés had trouble with the soldiers near Fort Laramie; and again in 1857 Inkpaduta massacred several families of settlers at Spirit Lake, Iowa. Finally, in 1862, the Minnesota Sioux, goaded by many wrongs, arose and murdered many of the settlers, afterward fleeing into the country of the Unkpapas and appealing to them for help, urging that all Indians should make common cause against the invader. This brought Sitting Bull face to face with a question which was not yet fully matured in his own mind; but having satisfied himself of the justice of their cause, he joined forces with the renegades during the summer of 1863, and from this time on he was an acknowledged leader.

In 1865 and 1866 he met the Canadian half-breed, Louis Riel, instigator of two rebellions, who had come across the line for safety; and in fact at this time he harbored a number of outlaws and fugitives from justice. His conversations with these, especially with the French mixed-bloods, who inflamed his prejudices against the Americans, all had their influence in making of the wily Sioux a determined enemy to the white man. While among his own people he was always affable and genial, he became boastful and domineer-

ing in his dealings with the hated race.
He once remarked that "if we wish to
make any impression upon the pale-face,
it is necessary to put on his mask."

Sitting Bull joined in the attack on
Fort Phil Kearny and in the subsequent
hostilities; but he accepted in good faith
the treaty of 1868, and soon after it was
signed he visited Washington with Red
Cloud and Spotted Tail, on which occasion
the three distinguished chiefs attracted
much attention and were entertained at
dinner by President Grant and other no-
tables. He considered that the life of the
white man as he saw it was no life for his
people, but hoped by close adherence to
the terms of this treaty to preserve the Big
Horn and Black Hills country for a per-
manent hunting ground. When gold was
discovered and the irrepressible gold
seekers made their historic dash across
the plains into this forbidden paradise,
then his faith in the white man's honor
was gone forever, and he took his final

SITTING BULL

and most persistent stand in defense of his nation and home. His bitter and at the same time well-grounded and philosophical dislike of the conquering race is well expressed in a speech made before the purely Indian council before referred to, upon the Powder River. I will give it in brief as it has been several times repeated to me by men who were present.

"Behold, my friends, the spring is come; the earth has gladly received the embraces of the sun, and we shall soon see the results of their love! Every seed is awakened, and all animal life. It is through this mysterious power that we too have our being, and we therefore yield to our neighbors, even to our animal neighbors, the same right as ourselves to inhabit this vast land.

"Yet hear me, friends! we have now to deal with another people, small and feeble when our forefathers first met with them, but now great and overbearing. Strangely enough, they have a mind to till the soil,

and the love of possessions is a disease in
them. These people have made many
rules that the rich may break, but the poor
may not! They have a religion in which
the poor worship, but the rich will not!
They even take tithes of the poor and
weak to support the rich and those who
rule. They claim this mother of ours,
the Earth, for their own use, and fence
their neighbors away from her, and de-
face her with their buildings and their
refuse. They compel her to produce out
of season, and when sterile she is made to
take medicine in order to produce again.
All this is sacrilege.

"This nation is like a spring freshet;
it overruns its banks and destroys all
who are in its path. We cannot dwell
side by side. Only seven years ago we
made a treaty by which we were assured
that the buffalo country should be left to
us forever. Now they threaten to take
that from us also. My brothers, shall we
submit? or shall we say to them: 'First

kill me, before you can take possession of
my fatherland!'"

As Sitting Bull spoke, so he felt, and he
had the courage to stand by his words.
Crazy Horse led his forces in the field; as
for him, he applied his energies to state
affairs, and by his strong and aggressive
personality contributed much to holding
the hostiles together.

It may be said without fear of contradic-
tion that Sitting Bull never killed any women
or children. He was a fair fighter, and
while not prominent in battle after his young
manhood, he was the brains of the Sioux resistance. He has been called a "medicine
man" and a "dreamer." Strictly speaking,
he was neither of these, and the white historians are prone to confuse the two. A
medicine man is a doctor or healer; a
dreamer is an active war prophet who leads
his war party according to his dream or
prophecy. What is called by whites "making medicine" in war time is again a wrong
conception. Every warrior carries a bag of

sacred or lucky charms, supposed to protect the wearer alone, but it has nothing to do with the success or safety of the party as a whole. No one can make any "medicine" to affect the result of a battle, although it has been said that Sitting Bull did this at the battle of the Little Big Horn.

When Custer and Reno attacked the camp at both ends, the chief was caught napping. The village was in danger of surprise, and the women and children must be placed in safety. Like other men of his age, Sitting Bull got his family together for flight, and then joined the warriors on the Reno side of the attack. Thus he was not in the famous charge against Custer; nevertheless, his voice was heard exhorting the warriors throughout that day.

During the autumn of 1876, after the fall of Custer, Sitting Bull was hunted all through the Yellowstone region by the military. The following characteristic letter, doubtless written at his dictation by a half-breed interpreter, was sent to Colonel Otis immediately after a daring attack upon his wagon train.

"I want to know what you are doing, traveling on this road. You scare all the buffalo away. I want to hunt in this place. I want you to turn back from here. If you don't, I will fight you again. I want you to leave what you have got here and turn back from here.

I am your friend
Sitting Bull.

I mean all the rations you have got and some powder. Wish you would write me as soon as you can."

Otis, however, kept on and joined Colonel Miles, who followed Sitting Bull with about four hundred soldiers. He overtook him at last on Cedar Creek, near the Yellowstone, and the two met midway between the lines for a parley. The army report says: "Sitting Bull wanted

peace in his own way." The truth was
that he wanted nothing more than had
been guaranteed to them by the treaty of
1868 — the exclusive possession of their
last hunting ground. This the government was not now prepared to grant, as
it had been decided to place all the Indians under military control upon the
various reservations.

Since it was impossible to reconcile two
such conflicting demands, the hostiles were
driven about from pillar to post for several
more years, and finally took refuge across
the line in Canada, where Sitting Bull
had placed his last hope of justice and
freedom for his race. Here he was joined
from time to time by parties of malcon-
tents from the reservation, driven largely
by starvation and ill-treatment to seek
another home. Here, too, they were followed by United States commissioners,
headed by General Terry, who endeavored
to persuade him to return, promising abundance of food and fair treatment, despite

the fact that the exiles were well aware
of the miserable condition of the "good
Indians" upon the reservations. He first
refused to meet them at all, and only did
so when advised to that effect by Major
Walsh of the Canadian mounted police.
This was his characteristic remark: "If
you have one honest man in Washington,
send him here and I will talk to him."

Sitting Bull was not moved by fair
words; but when he found that if they
had liberty on that side, they had little
else, that the Canadian government would
give them protection but no food; that
the buffalo had been all but exterminated
and his starving people were already beginning to desert him, he was compelled
at last, in 1881, to report at Fort Buford,
North Dakota, with his band of hungry,
homeless, and discouraged refugees. It
was, after all, to hunger and not to the
strong arm of the military that he surrendered in the end.

In spite of the invitation that had been

extended to him in the name of the "Great Father" at Washington, he was immediately thrown into a military prison, and afterward handed over to Colonel Cody ("Buffalo Bill") as an advertisement for his "Wild West Show." After traveling about for several years with the famous showman, thus increasing his knowledge of the weaknesses as well as the strength of the white man, the deposed and humiliated chief settled down quietly with his people upon the Standing Rock agency in North Dakota, where his immediate band occupied the Grand River district and set to raising cattle and horses. They made good progress; much better, in fact, than that of the "coffee-coolers" or "loafer" Indians, received the missionaries kindly and were soon a church-going people.

When the Commissions of 1888 and 1889 came to treat with the Sioux for a further cession of land and a reduction of their reservations, nearly all were opposed to consent on any terms. Nevertheless, by hook or by crook, enough signatures were finally obtained to carry the measure through, although it is said that many were those of women and the so-called "squaw-men", who had no rights in the land. At the same time, rations were cut down, and there was general hardship and dissatisfaction. Crazy Horse was long since dead; Spotted Tail had fallen at the hands of one of his own tribe; Red Cloud had become a feeble old man, and the disaffected among the Sioux began once more to look to Sitting Bull for leadership.

At this crisis a strange thing happened. A half-breed Indian in Nevada promulgated the news that the Messiah had appeared to him upon a peak in the Rockies, dressed in rabbit skins, and bringing a message to the red race. The message was to the effect that since his first coming had been in vain, since the white people had doubted and reviled him, had nailed him to the cross, and trampled upon his doctrines, he had come again in pity to save the Indian. He declared that he would cause the earth to shake and to overthrow the cities of the whites and destroy them, that the buffalo would return, and the land belong to the red race forever! These events were to come to pass within two years; and meanwhile they were to prepare for his coming by the ceremonies and dances which he commanded.

This curious story spread like wildfire and met with eager acceptance among the suffering and discontented people. The teachings of Christian missionaries had prepared them to believe in a Messiah, and the prescribed ceremonial was much more in accord with their traditions than the conventional worship of the churches. Chiefs of many tribes sent delegations to the Indian prophet; Short Bull, Kicking Bear, and others went from among the Sioux, and on their return all inaugurated the dances at once. There was an attempt at first to keep the matter secret, but it soon became generally known and seriously disconcerted the Indian agents and others, who were quick to suspect a hostile conspiracy under all this religious enthusiasm. As a matter of fact, there was no thought of an uprising; the dancing was innocent enough, and pathetic enough their despairing hope in a pitiful Saviour who should overwhelm their oppressors and bring back their golden age.

When the Indians refused to give up the "Ghost Dance" at the bidding of the authorities, the growing suspicion and alarm focused upon Sitting Bull, who in spirit had never been any too submissive, and it was determined to order his arrest. At the special request of Major McLaughlin, agent at Standing Rock, forty of his Indian police were sent out to Sitting Bull's home on Grand River to secure his person (followed at some little distance by a body of United States troops for reinforcement, in case of trouble). These police are enlisted from among the tribesmen at each agency, and have proved uniformly brave and faithful. They entered the cabin at daybreak, aroused the chief from a sound slumber, helped him to dress, and led him unresisting from the house; but when he came out in the gray dawn of that December morning in 1890, to find his cabin surrounded by armed men and himself led away to he knew not what fate, he cried out loudly :

"They have taken me : what say you to it ?"

Men poured out of the neighboring houses, and in a few minutes the police were themselves surrounded with an excited and rapidly increasing throng. They harangued the crowd in vain ; Sitting Bull's blood was up, and he again appealed to his men. His adopted brother, the Assiniboine captive whose life he had saved so many years before, was the first to fire. His shot killed Lieutenant Bull Head, who held Sitting Bull by the arm. Then there was a short but sharp conflict, in which Sitting Bull and six of his defenders and

six of the Indian police were slain, with
many more wounded. The chief's young
son, Crow Foot, and his devoted "brother"
died with him. When all was over, and the
terrified people had fled precipitately across
the river, the soldiers appeared upon the
brow of the long hill and fired their Hotch-
kiss guns into the deserted camp.

Thus ended the life of a natural strategist of no mean courage and ability. The
great chief was buried without honors
outside the cemetery at the post, and for
some years the grave was marked by a
mere board at its head. Recently some
women have built a cairn of rocks there
in token of respect and remembrance.

RAIN-IN-THE-FACE

T HE noted Sioux warrior, Rain-in-the-Face, whose name once carried terror to every part of the frontier, died at his home on the Standing Rock reserve in North Dakota on September 14, 1905. About two months before his death I went to see him for the last time, where he lay upon the bed of sickness from which he never rose again, and drew from him his life-history.

It had been my experience that you cannot induce an Indian to tell a story, or even his own name, by asking him directly.

"Friend," I said, "even if a man is on a hot trail, he stops for a smoke! In the good old days, before the charge there was a smoke. At home, by the fireside, when the old men were asked to tell their brave deeds, again the pipe was passed. So come, let us smoke now to the memory of the old days!"

He took of my tobacco and filled his long pipe, and we smoked. Then I told an old mirthful story to get him in the humor of relating his own history.

The old man lay upon an iron bedstead, covered by a red blanket, in a corner of the little log cabin. He was all alone that day; only an old dog lay silent and watchful at his master's feet.

Finally he looked up and said with a pleasant smile:

"True, friend; it is the old custom to retrace one's trail before leaving it forever! I know that I am at the door of the spirit home.

"I was born near the forks of the Cheyenne River, about seventy years ago. My father was not a chief; my grandfather was not a chief, but a good hunter and a feast-maker. On my mother's side I had some noted ancestors, but they left me no chieftainship. I had to work for my reputation.

"When I was a boy, I loved to fight," he

continued. "In all our boyish games I had
the name of being hard to handle, and I took
much pride in the fact.

"I was about ten years old when we
encountered a band of Cheyennes. They
were on friendly terms with us, but we boys
always indulged in sham fights on such
occasions, and this time I got in an honest
fight with a Cheyenne boy older than I.   I
got the best of the boy, but he hit me hard
in the face several times, and my face was
all spattered with blood and streaked where
the paint had been washed away. The
Sioux boys whooped and yelled :

"'His enemy is down, and his face is
spattered as if with rain ! Rain-in-the-
Face ! His name shall be Rain-in-the-
Face !'

"Afterwards, when I was a young man,
we went on a warpath against the Gros
Ventres. We stole some of their horses,
but were overtaken and had to abandon
the horses and fight for our lives. I had
wished my face to represent the sun when

partly covered with darkness, so I painted it half black, half red. We fought all day in the rain, and my face was partly washed and streaked with red and black: so again I was christened Rain-in-the-Face. We considered it an honorable name.

"I had been on many warpaths, but was not especially successful until about the time the Sioux began to fight with the white man. One of the most daring attacks that we ever made was at Fort Totten, North Dakota, in the summer of 1866.

"Hóhay, the Assiniboine captive of Sitting Bull, was the leader in this raid. Wapáypay, the Fearless Bear, who was afterward hanged at Yankton, was the bravest man among us. He dared Hóhay to make the charge. Hóhay accepted the challenge, and in turn dared the other to ride with him through the agency and right under the walls of the fort, which was well garrisoned and strong.

"Wapáypay and I in those days called each other 'brother-friend.' It was a life-

and-death vow. What one does the other must do; and that meant that I must be in the forefront of the charge, and if he is killed, I must fight until I die also!

"I prepared for death. I painted as usual like an eclipse of the sun, half black and half red."

His eyes gleamed and his face lighted up remarkably as he talked, pushing his black hair back from his forehead with a nervous gesture.

"Now the signal for the charge was given! I started even with Wapáypay, but his horse was faster than mine, so he left me a little behind as we neared the fort. This was bad for me, for by that time the soldiers had somewhat recovered from the surprise and were aiming better.

"Their big gun talked very loud, but my Wapáypay was leading on, leaning forward on his fleet pony like a flying squirrel on a smooth log! He held his rawhide shield on the right side, a little to the front, and so did I. Our warwhoop was like the coyotes singing in the evening, when they smell blood!

"The soldiers' guns talked fast, but few were hurt. Their big gun was like a toothless old dog, who only makes himself hotter the more noise he makes," he remarked with some humor.

"How much harm we did I do not know, but we made things lively for a time; and the white men acted as people do when a swarm of angry bees get into camp. We made a successful retreat, but some of the reservation Indians followed us yelling, until Hóhay told them that he did not wish to fight with the captives of the white man, for there would be no honor in that. There was blood running down my leg, and I found that both my horse and I were slightly wounded.

"Some two years later we attacked a fort west of the Black Hills [Fort Phil Kearny, Wyoming]. It was there we killed one hundred soldiers." [The military reports say eighty men, under the command of

Captain Fetterman — not one left alive to tell the tale!]   "Nearly every band of the Sioux nation was represented in that fight — Red Cloud, Spotted Tail, Crazy Horse, Sitting Bull, Big Foot, and all our great chiefs were there.   Of course such men as I were then comparatively unknown. However, there were many noted young warriors, among them Sword, the younger Young-Man-Afraid, American Horse [afterward chief], Crow King, and others.

"This was the plan decided upon after many councils.   The main war party lay in ambush, and a few of the bravest young men were appointed to attack the woodchoppers who were cutting logs to complete the building of the fort.   We were told not to kill these men, but to chase them into the fort and retreat slowly, defying the white men; and if the soldiers should follow, we were to lead them into the ambush.   They took our bait exactly as we had hoped! It was a matter of a very few minutes, for every soldier lay dead in a shorter time than it takes to annihilate a small herd of buffalo.

"This attack was hastened because most of the Sioux on the Missouri River and eastward had begun to talk of suing for peace. But even this did not stop the peace movement. The very next year a treaty was signed at Fort Rice, Dakota Territory, by nearly all the Sioux chiefs, in which it was agreed on the part of the Great Father in Washington that all the country north of the Republican River in Nebraska, including the Black Hills and the Big Horn Mountains, was to be always Sioux country, and no white man should intrude upon it without our permission. Even with this agreement Sitting Bull and Crazy Horse were not satisfied, and they would not sign.

"Up to this time I had fought in some important battles, but had achieved no great deed. I was ambitious to make a name for myself. I joined war parties against the Crows, Mandans, Gros Ventres, and Pawnees, and gained some little distinction.

"It was when the white men found the yellow metal in our country, and came in great numbers, driving away our game, that we took up arms against them for the last time. I must say here that the chiefs who were loudest for war were among the first to submit and accept reservation life. Spotted Tail was a great warrior, yet he was one of the first to yield, because he was promised by the Chief Soldiers that they would make him chief of all the Sioux. Ugh! he would have stayed with Sitting Bull to the last had it not been for his ambition.

"About this time we young warriors began to watch the trails of the white men into the Black Hills, and when we saw a wagon coming we would hide at the crossing and kill them all without much trouble. We did this to discourage the whites from coming into our country without our permission. It was the duty of our Great Father at Washington, by the agreement of 1868, to keep his white children away.

"During the troublesome time after this treaty, which no one seemed to respect, either white or Indian [but the whites broke it first], I was like many other young men — much on the warpath, but with little honor. I had not yet become noted for any great deed. Finally, Wapáypay and I waylaid and killed a white soldier on his way from the fort to his home in the east.

"There were a few Indians who were liars, and never on the warpath, playing 'good Indian' with the Indian agents and the war chiefs at the forts. Some of this faithless set betrayed me, and told more than I ever did. I was seized and taken to the fort near Bismarck, North Dakota [Fort Abraham Lincoln], by a brother [Tom Custer] of the Long-Haired War Chief, and imprisoned there. These same lying Indians, who were selling their services as scouts to the white man, told me that I was to be shot to death, or else hanged upon a tree. I answered that I was not afraid to die.

"However, there was an old soldier who

used to bring my food and stand guard over
me — he was a white man, it is true, but he
had an Indian heart! He came to me one
day and unfastened the iron chain and ball
with which they had locked my leg, saying
by signs and what little Sioux he could
muster :

"'Go, friend! take the chain and ball with
you. I shall shoot, but the voice of the gun
will lie.'

"When he had made me understand, you
may guess that I ran my best! I was almost
over the bank when he fired his piece at me
several times, but I had already gained cover
and was safe. I have never told this before,
and would not, lest it should do him an injury, but he was an old man then, and I am
sure he must be dead long since. That old
soldier taught me that some of the white
people have hearts," he added, quite seriously.

"I went back to Standing Rock in the
night, and I had to hide for several days in
the woods, where food was brought to me

by my relatives. The Indian police were ordered to retake me, and they pretended to hunt for me, but really they did not, for if they had found me I would have died with one or two of them, and they knew it! In a few days I departed with several others, and we rejoined the hostile camp on the Powder River and made some trouble for the men who were building the great iron track north of us [Northern Pacific].

"In the spring the hostile Sioux got together again upon the Tongue River. It was one of the greatest camps of the Sioux that I ever saw. There were some Northern Cheyennes with us, under Two Moon, and a few Santee Sioux, renegades from Canada, under Inkpaduta, who had killed white people in Iowa long before. We had decided to fight the white soldiers until no warrior should be left."

At this point Rain-in-the-Face took up his tobacco pouch and began again to fill his pipe.

"Of course the younger warriors were delighted with the prospect of a great fight!

Our scouts had discovered piles of oats for horses and other supplies near the Missouri River. They had been brought by the white man's fire-boats. Presently they reported a great army about a day's travel to the south, with Shoshone and Crow scouts.

"There was excitement among the people, and a great council was held. Many spoke. I was asked the condition of those Indians who had gone upon the reservation, and I told them truly that they were nothing more than prisoners. It was decided to go out and meet Three Stars [General Crook] at a safe distance from our camp.

"We met him on the Little Rosebud. I believe that if we had waited and allowed him to make the attack, he would have fared no better than Custer. He was too strongly fortified where he was, and I think, too, that he was saved partly by his Indian allies, for the scouts discovered us first and fought us first, thus giving him time to make his preparations. I think he was more wise than brave! After we had left that neighborhood he might have pushed on and connected with the Long-Haired Chief. That would have saved Custer and perhaps won the day.

"When we crossed from Tongue River to the Little Big Horn, on account of the scarcity of game, we did not anticipate any more trouble. Our runners had discovered that Crook had retraced his trail to Goose Creek, and we did not suppose that the white men would care to follow us farther into the rough country.

"Suddenly the Long-Haired Chief appeared with his men! It was a surprise."

"What part of the camp were you in when the soldiers attacked the lower end?" I asked.

"I had been invited to a feast at one of the young men's lodges [a sort of club]. There was a certain warrior who was making preparations to go against the Crows, and I had decided to go also," he said.

"While I was eating my meat we heard the war cry! We all rushed out, and saw a warrior riding at top speed from the lower camp, giving the warning as he came. Then we heard the reports of the soldiers' guns, which sounded differently from the guns fired by our people in battle.

"I ran to my teepee and seized my gun, a bow, and a quiver full of arrows. I already had my stone war club, for you know we usually carry those by way of ornament. Just as I was about to set out to meet Reno, a body of soldiers appeared nearly opposite us, at the edge of a long line of cliffs across the river.

"All of us who were mounted and ready immediately started down the stream toward the ford. There were Ogallalas, Minneconjous, Cheyennes, and some Unkpapas, and those around me seemed to be nearly all very young men.

"'Behold, there is among us a young woman!' I shouted. 'Let no young man hide behind her garment!' I knew that would make those young men brave.

"The woman was Tashenamani, or Moving Robe, whose brother had just been killed in the fight with Three Stars. Holding her brother's war staff over her head, and leaning forward upon her charger, she looked as pretty as a bird. Always when there is a woman in the charge, it causes the warriors to vie with one another in displaying their valor," he added.

"The foremost warriors had almost surrounded the white men, and more were continually crossing the stream. The soldiers had dismounted, and were firing into the camp from the top of the cliff."

"My friend, was Sitting Bull in this fight?" I inquired.

"I did not see him there, but I learned afterward that he was among those who met Reno, and that was three or four of the white man's miles from Custer's position. Later he joined the attack upon Custer, but was not among the foremost.

"When the troops were surrounded on two sides, with the river on the third, the order came to charge! There were many very

young men, some of whom had only a war
staff or a stone war club in hand, who
plunged into the column, knocking the men
over and stampeding their horses.

"The soldiers had mounted and started
back, but when the onset came they dismounted again and separated into several
divisions, facing different ways. They fired
as fast as they could load their guns, while
we used chiefly arrows and war clubs.
There seemed to be two distinct movements
among the Indians. One body moved
continually in a circle, while the other rode
directly into and through the troops.

"Presently some of the soldiers re-
mounted and fled along the ridge toward
Reno's position; but they were followed by
our warriors, like hundreds of blackbirds
after a hawk. A larger body remained
together at the upper end of a little ravine,
and fought bravely until they were cut to
pieces. I had always thought that white
men were cowards, but I had a great respect
for them after this day.

"It is generally said that a young man with nothing but a war staff in his hand broke through the column and knocked down the leader very early in the fight. We supposed him to be the leader, be-cause he stood up in full view, swinging his big knife [sword] over his head, and talking loud. Some one unknown afterwards shot the chief, and he was probably killed also; for if not, he would have told of the deed, and called others to witness it. So it is that no one knows who killed the Long-Haired Chief [General Custer].

"After the first rush was over, *coups* were counted as usual on the bodies of the slain. You know four *coups* [or blows] can be counted on the body of an enemy, and who-ever counts the first one [touches it for the first time] is entitled to the 'first feather.'

"There was an Indian here called Appear-ing Elk, who died a short time ago. He was slightly wounded in the charge. He had some of the weapons of the Long-Haired Chief, and the Indians used to say jokingly after we came upon the reservation that Appearing Elk must have killed the Chief, because he had his sword! However, the scramble for plunder did not begin until all were dead. I do not think he killed Custer, and if he had, the time to claim the honor was immediately after the fight.

"Many lies have been told of me. Some say that I killed the Chief, and others that I cut out the heart of his brother [Tom Custer], because he had caused me to be imprisoned. Why, in that fight the excitement was so great that we scarcely recognized our nearest friends! Everything was done like lightning. After the battle we young men were chasing horses all over the prairie, while the old men and women plundered the bodies; and if any mutilating was done, it was by the old men.

"I have lived peaceably ever since we came upon the reservation. No one can say that Rain-in-the-Face has broken the rules of the Great Father. I fought for my

people and my country. When we were
conquered I remained silent, as a warrior
should. Rain-in-the-Face was killed when
he put down his weapons before the Great
Father. His spirit was gone then; only
his poor body lived on, but now it is almost
ready to lie down for the last time. Ho,
hechetu! [It is well.]"

TWO STRIKE

IT is a pity that so many interesting names of well-known Indians have been mistranslated, so that their meaning becomes very vague if it is not wholly lost. In some cases an opposite meaning is conveyed. For instance there is the name, "Young-Man-Afraid-of-His-Horses." It does not mean that the owner of the name is afraid of his own horse — far from it! Tashunkekokipapi signifies "The young men [of the enemy] fear his horses." Whenever that man attacks, the enemy knows there will be a determined charge.

The name Tashunkewitko, or Crazy Horse, is a poetic simile. This leader was likened to an untrained or untouched horse, wild, ignorant of domestic uses, splendid in action, and unconscious of danger.

The name of Two Strike is a deed name.

In a battle with the Utes this man knocked two enemies from the back of a war horse. The true rendering of the name Nomkahpa would be, "He knocked off two."

I was well acquainted with Two Strike and spent many pleasant hours with him, both at Washington, D. C., and in his home on the Rosebud reservation. What I have written is not all taken from his own mouth, because he was modest in talking about himself, but I had him vouch for the truth of the stories. He said that he was born near the Republican River about 1832. His earliest recollection was of an attack by the Shoshones upon their camp on the Little Piney. The first white men he ever met were traders who visited his people when he was very young. The incident was still vividly with him, because, he said, "They made my father crazy," [drunk]. This made a deep impression upon him, he told me, so that from that day he was always afraid of the white man's "mysterious water."

Two Strike was not a large man, but he was very supple and alert in motion, as agile as an antelope. His face was mobile and intelligent. Although he had the usual somber visage of an Indian, his expression brightened up wonderfully when he talked. In some ways wily and shrewd in intellect, he was not deceitful nor mean. He had a high sense of duty and honor. Patriotism was his ideal and goal of life.

As a young man he was modest and even shy, although both his father and grandfather were well-known chiefs. I could find few noteworthy incidents in his early life, save that he was an expert rider of wild horses. At one time I was pressing him to give me some interesting incident of his boyhood. He replied to the effect that there was plenty of excitement but "not much in it." There was a delegation of Sioux chiefs visiting Washington, and we were spending an evening together in their hotel. Hollow Horn Bear spoke up and said:

"Why don't you tell him how you and a buffalo cow together held your poor father up and froze him almost to death?"

Everybody laughed, and another man remarked: "I think he had better tell the medicine man (meaning myself) how he lost the power of speech when he first tried to court a girl." Two Strike, although he was then close to eighty years of age, was visibly embarrassed by their chaff.

"Anyway, I stuck to the trail. I kept on till I got what I wanted," he muttered. And then came the story.

The old chief, his father, was very fond of the buffalo hunt; and being accomplished in horsemanship and a fine shot, although not very powerfully built, young Two Strike was already following hard in his footsteps. Like every proud father, his was giving him every incentive to perfect his skill, and one day challenged his sixteen-year-old son to the feat of "one arrow to kill" at the very next chase.

It was midwinter. A large herd of

buffalo was reported by the game scout.
The hunters gathered at daybreak prepared for the charge. The old chief had
his tried charger equipped with a soft,
pillow-like Indian saddle and a lariat.
His old sinew-backed hickory bow was
examined and strung, and a fine straight
arrow with a steel head carefully selected
for the test. He adjusted a keen butcher
knife over his leather belt, which held a
warm buffalo robe securely about his body.
He wore neither shirt nor coat, although a
piercing wind was blowing from the northwest. The youthful Two Strike had his
favorite bow and his swift pony, which was
perhaps dearer to him than his closest boy
comrade.

Now the hunters crouched upon their
horses' necks like an army in line of battle,
while behind them waited the boys and old
men with pack ponies to carry the meat.
"Hukahey!" shouted the leader as a warning. "Yekiya wo!" (Go) and in an instant all the ponies leaped forward against

the cutting wind, as if it were the start in a horse race. Every rider leaned forward, tightly wrapped in his robe, watching the flying herd for an opening in the mass of buffalo, a chance to cut out some of the fattest cows. This was the object of the race.

The chief had a fair start; his horse was well trained and needed no urging nor guidance. Without the slightest pull on the lariat he dashed into the thickest of the herd. The youth's pony had been prancing and rearing impatiently; he started a little behind, yet being swift passed many. His rider had one clear glimpse of his father ahead of him, then the snow arose in blinding clouds on the trail of the bison. The whoops of the hunters, the lowing of the cows, and the menacing glances of the bulls as they plunged along, or now and then stood at bay, were enough to unnerve a boy less well tried. He was unable to select his victim. He had been carried deeply into the midst of the herd and found himself helpless to make the one sure shot, therefore he held his one arrow in his mouth and merely strove to separate them so as to get his chance.

At last the herd parted, and he cut out two fat cows, and was maneuvering for position when a rider appeared out of the snow cloud on their other side. This aroused him to make haste lest his rival secure both cows; he saw his chance, and in a twinkling his arrow sped clear through one of the animals so that she fell headlong.

In this instant he observed that the man who had joined him was his own father, who had met with the same difficulties as himself. When the young man had shot his only arrow, the old chief with a whoop went after the cow that was left, but as he gained her broadside, his horse stepped in a badger hole and fell, throwing him headlong. The maddened buffalo, as sometimes happens in such cases, turned upon the pony and gored him to death. His rider lay motionless, while Two Strike rushed for-

ward to draw her attention, but she merely
tossed her head at him, while persistently
standing guard over the dead horse and the
all but frozen Indian.

Alas for the game of "one arrow to kill!"
The boy must think fast, for his father's
robe had slipped off, and he was playing
dead, lying almost naked in the bitter air
upon the trampled snow. His bluff would
not serve, so he flew back to pull out his
solitary arrow from the body of the dead
cow. Quickly wheeling again, he sent it
into her side and she fell. The one arrow
to kill had become one arrow to kill two
buffalo! At the council lodge that evening
Two Strike was the hero.

The following story is equally characteristic of him, and in explanation it should be
said that in the good old days among the
Sioux, a young man is not supposed to
associate with girls until he is ready to take
a wife. It was a rule with our young men,
especially the honorable and well-born, to
gain some reputation in the hunt and in

war, — the more difficult the feats achieved the better, — before even speaking to a young woman. Many a life was risked in the effort to establish a reputation along these lines. Courtship was no secret, but rather a social event, often celebrated by the proud parents with feasts and presents to the poor, and this etiquette was sometimes felt by a shy or sensitive youth as an insurmountable obstacle to the fulfilment of his desires.

Two Strike was the son and grandson of a chief, but he could not claim any credit for the deeds of his forbears. He had not only to guard their good name but achieve one for himself. This he had set out to do, and he did well. He was now of marriageable age with a war record, and admitted to the council, yet he did not seem to trouble himself at all about a wife. His was strictly a bachelor career. Meanwhile, as is apt to be the case, his parents had thought much about a possible daughter-in-law, and had even collected ponies, fine robes, and other

acceptable goods to be given away in honor
of the event, whenever it should take place.
Now and then they would drop a sly hint,
but with no perceptible effect.

They did not and could not know of the
inward struggle that racked his mind at this
period of his life. The shy and modest
young man was dying for a wife, yet could
not bear even to think of speaking to a
young woman! The fearless hunter of
buffaloes, mountain lions, and grizzlies, the
youth who had won his eagle feathers in a
battle with the Utes, could not bring himself to take this tremendous step.

At last his father appealed to him directly. "My son," he declared, "it is your
duty to take unto yourself a wife, in order
that the honors won by your ancestors and
by yourself may be handed down in the
direct line. There are several eligible young
women in our band whose parents have
intimated a wish to have you for their
son-in-law."

Two Strike made no reply, but he was

greatly disturbed. He had no wish to have the old folks select his bride, for if the truth were told, his choice was already made. He had simply lacked the courage to go a-courting!

The next morning, after making an unusually careful toilet, he took his best horse and rode to a point overlooking the path by which the girls went for water. Here the young men were wont to take their stand, and, if fortunate, intercept the girl of their heart for a brief but fateful interview. Two Strike had determined to speak straight to the point, and as soon as he saw the pretty maid he came forward boldly and placed himself in her way. A long moment passed. She glanced up at him shyly but not without encouragement. His teeth fairly chattered with fright, and he could not say a word. She looked again, noted his strange looks, and believed him suddenly taken ill. He appeared to be suffering. At last he feebly made signs for her to go on and leave him alone. The maiden was sympathetic, but as she did not know what else to do she obeyed his request.

The poor youth was so ashamed of his cowardice that he afterward admitted his first thought was to take his own life. He believed he had disgraced himself forever in the eyes of the only girl he had ever loved. However, he determined to conquer his weakness and win her, which he did. The story came out many years after and was told with much enjoyment by the old men.

Two Strike was better known by his own people than by the whites, for he was individually a terror in battle rather than a leader. He achieved his honorable name in a skirmish with the Utes in Colorado. The Sioux regarded these people as their bravest enemies, and the outcome of the fight was for some time uncertain. First the Sioux were forced to retreat and then their opponents, and at the latter point the horse of a certain Ute was shot under him. A friend came to his rescue and took him up behind him. Our hero overtook them

in flight, raised his war club, and knocked
both men off with one blow.

He was a very old man when he died, only
two or three years ago, on the Rosebud
reservation.

AMERICAN HORSE

O NE of the wittiest and shrewdest of the Sioux chiefs was American Horse, who succeeded to the name and position of an uncle, killed in the battle of Slim Buttes in 1876. The younger American Horse was born a little before the encroachments of the whites upon the Sioux country became serious and their methods aggressive, and his early manhood brought him into that most trying and critical period of our history. He had been tutored by his uncle, since his own father was killed in battle while he was still very young. The American Horse band was closely attached to a trading post, and its members in consequence were inclined to be friendly with the whites, a policy closely adhered to by their leader.

When he was born, his old grandfather

said: "Put him out in the sun! Let him ask his great-grandfather, the Sun, for the warm blood of a warrior!" And he had warm blood. He was a genial man, liking notoriety and excitement. He always seized an opportunity to leap into the center of the arena.

In early life he was a clownish sort of boy among the boys — an expert mimic and impersonator. This talent made him popular and in his way a leader. He was a natural actor, and early showed marked ability as a speaker.

American Horse was about ten years old when he was attacked by three Crow warriors, while driving a herd of ponies to water. Here he displayed native cunning and initiative. It seemed he had scarcely a chance to escape, for the enemy was near. He yelled frantically at the ponies to start them toward home, while he dropped off into a thicket of willows and hid there. A part of the herd was caught in sight of the camp and there was a counter chase, but

AMERICAN HORSE

the Crows got away with the ponies. Of course his mother was frantic, believing her boy had been killed or captured; but after the excitement was over, he appeared in camp unhurt. When questioned about his escape, he remarked: "I knew they would not take the time to hunt for small game when there was so much bigger close by."

When he was quite a big boy, he joined in a buffalo hunt, and on the way back with the rest of the hunters his mule became unmanageable. American Horse had insisted on riding him in addition to a heavy load of meat and skins, and the animal evidently resented this, for he suddenly began to run and kick, scattering fresh meat along the road, to the merriment of the crowd. But the boy turned actor, and made it appear that it was at his wish the mule had given this diverting performance. He clung to the back of his plunging and braying mount like a circus rider, singing a Brave Heart song, and finally brought up amid the laughter and cheers of his com-

panions. Far from admitting defeat, he
boasted of his horsemanship and declared
that his "brother" the donkey would put
any enemy to flight, and that they should
be called upon to lead a charge.

It was several years later that he went to
sleep early one night and slept soundly,
having been scouting for two nights pre-
vious. It happened that there was a raid
by the Crows, and when he awoke in the
midst of the yelling and confusion, he
sprang up and attempted to join in the
fighting. Everybody knew his voice in all
the din, so when he fired his gun and announced a coup, as was the custom, others
rushed to the spot, to find that he had shot
a hobbled pony belonging to their own camp.
The laugh was on him, and he never recovered from his chagrin at this mistake. In
fact, although he was undoubtedly fearless
and tried hard to distinguish himself in
warfare, he did not succeed.

It is told of him that he once went with
a war party of young men to the Wind

River country against the Shoshones. At
last they discovered a large camp, but there
were only a dozen or so of the Sioux, therefore they hid themselves and watched for
their opportunity to attack an isolated party
of hunters. While waiting thus, they ran
short of food. One day a small party of
Shoshones was seen near at hand, and in the
midst of the excitement and preparations
for the attack, young American Horse
caught sight of a fat black-tail deer close by.
Unable to resist the temptation, he pulled
an arrow from his quiver and sent it through
the deer's heart, then with several of his
half-starved companions sprang upon the
yet quivering body of the animal to cut out
the liver, which was sometimes eaten raw.
One of the men was knocked down, it is
said, by the last kick of the dying buck, but
having swallowed a few mouthfuls the
warriors rushed upon and routed their
enemies. It is still told of American Horse
how he killed game and feasted between the
ambush and the attack.

At another time he was drying his sacred
war bonnet and other gear over a small fire.
These articles were held in great veneration
by the Indians and handled accordingly.
Suddenly the fire blazed up, and our hero so
far forgot himself as to begin energetically
beating out the flames with the war bonnet,
breaking off one of the sacred buffalo horns
in the act. One could almost fill a book
with his mishaps and exploits. I will give
one of them in his own words as well as I
can remember them.

"We were as promising a party of young
warriors as our tribe ever sent against any
of its ancestral enemies. It was mid-
summer, and after going two days' journey
from home we began to send two scouts
ahead daily while the main body kept a half
day behind. The scouts set out every
evening and traveled all night. One night
the great war pipe was held out to me and to
Young-Man-Afraid-of-His-Horses. At daybreak, having met no one, we hid our horses
and climbed to the top of the nearest butte

to take an observation.   It was a very hot day.   We lay flat on our blankets, facing the west where the cliff fell off in a sheer descent, and with our backs toward the more gradual slope dotted with scrub pines and cedars.   We stuck some tall grass on our heads and proceeded to study the landscape spread before us for any sign of man.

"The sweeping valleys were dotted with herds, both large and small, of buffalo and elk, and now and then we caught a glimpse of a coyote slinking into the gulches, returning from night hunting to sleep.   While intently watching some moving body at a distance, we could not yet tell whether of men or animals, I heard a faint noise behind me and slowly turned my head.   Behold! a grizzly bear sneaking up on all fours and almost ready to spring!

"'Run!' I yelled into the ear of my companion, and we both leaped to our feet in a second.   'Separate! separate!' he shouted, and as we did so, the bear chose me for his meat.   I ran downhill as fast as I could, but he was gaining. 'Dodge around a tree!' screamed Young-Man-Afraid. I took a deep breath and made a last spurt, desperately circling the first tree I came to. As the ground was steep just there, I turned a somersault one way and the bear the other. I picked myself up in time to climb the tree, and was fairly out of reach when he gathered himself together and came at me more furiously than ever, holding in one paw the shreds of my breechcloth, for in the fall he had just scratched my back and cut my belt in two, and carried off my only garment for a trophy!

"My friend was well up another tree and laughing heartily at my predicament, and when the bear saw that he could not get at either of us he reluctantly departed, after I had politely addressed him and promised to make an offering to his spirit on my safe return. I don't think I ever had a narrower escape," he concluded.

During the troublous times from 1865 to 1877, American Horse advocated yielding

to the government at any cost, being no
doubt convinced of the uselessness of resistance. He was not a recognized leader
until 1876, when he took the name and place
of his uncle. Up to this time he bore the
nickname of Manishnee (Can not walk, or
Played out.)

When the greater part of the Ogallalas,
to which band he belonged, came into the
reservation, he at once allied himself with
the peace element at the Red Cloud agency,
near Fort Robinson, Nebraska, and took no
small part in keeping the young braves
quiet. Since the older and better-known
chiefs, with the exception of Spotted Tail,
were believed to be hostile at heart, the military made much use of him. Many of his
young men enlisted as scouts by his advice,
and even he himself entered the service.

In the early part of the year 1876, there
was a rumor that certain bands were in
danger of breaking away. Their leader
was one Sioux Jim, so nicknamed by the
soldiers. American Horse went to him as

peacemaker, but was told he was a woman
and no brave. He returned to his own
camp and told his men that Sioux Jim
meant mischief, and in order to prevent
another calamity to the tribe, he must be
chastised. He again approached the warlike Jim with several warriors at his back.
The recalcitrant came out, gun in hand, but
the wily chief was too quick for him. He
shot and wounded the rebel, whereupon
one of his men came forward and killed him.

This quelled the people for the time being and up to the killing of Crazy Horse.
In the crisis precipitated by this event,
American Horse was again influential and
energetic in the cause of the government.
From this time on he became an active
participant in the affairs of the Teton
Sioux. He was noted for his eloquence,
which was nearly always conciliatory, yet
he could say very sharp things of the
duplicity of the whites. He had much ease
of manner and was a master of repartee.
I recall his saying that if you have got to

wear golden slippers to enter the white man's heaven no Indian will ever get there, as the whites have got the Black Hills and with them all the gold.

It was during the last struggle of his people, at the time of the Messiah craze in 1890–1891, that he demonstrated as never before the real greatness of the man. While many of his friends were carried away by the new thought, he held aloof from it and cautioned his band to do the same. When it developed into an extensive upheaval among the nations he took his positive stand against it.

Presently all Indians who did not dance the Ghost Dance were ordered to come into camp at Pine Ridge agency. American Horse was the first to bring in his people. I was there at the time and talked with him daily. When Little was arrested, it had been agreed among the disaffected to have him resist, which meant that he would be roughly handled. This was to be their excuse to attack the Indian police, which would probably lead to a general massacre or outbreak. I know that this desperate move was opposed from the beginning by American Horse, and it was believed that his life was threatened.

On the day of the "Big Issue", when thousands of Indians were gathered at the agency, this man Little, who had been in hiding, walked boldly among them. Of course the police would arrest him at sight, and he was led toward the guardhouse. He struggled with them, but was overpowered. A crowd of warriors rushed to his rescue, and there was confusion and a general shout of "Hurry up with them! Kill them all!" I saw American Horse walk out of the agent's office and calmly face the excited mob.

"What are you going to do?" he asked. "Stop, men, stop and think before you act! Will you murder your children, your women, yes, destroy your nation to-day?" He stood before them like a statue and the men who held the two policemen helpless paused for an instant. He went on: "You are brave to-day because you outnumber the white men, but what will you do to-morrow? There are railroads on all sides of you. The soldiers will pour in from every direction by thousands and surround you. You have little food or ammunition. It will be the end of your people. Stop, I say, stop now!"

Jack Red Cloud, son of the old chief, rushed up to him and thrust a revolver almost in his face. "It is you and men like you," he shouted, "who have reduced our race to slavery and starvation!" American Horse did not flinch but deliberately re-entered the office, followed by Jack still flourishing the pistol. But his timely appearance and eloquence had saved the day. Others of the police force had time to reach the spot, and with a large crowd of friendly Indians had taken command of the situation.

When I went into the office I found him alone but apparently quite calm. "Where are the agent and the clerks?" I asked.

"They fled by the back door," he replied, smiling. "I think they are in the cellar. These fools outside had almost caught us asleep, but I think it is over now."

American Horse was one of the earliest advocates of education for the Indian, and his son Samuel and nephew Robert were among the first students at Carlisle. I think one or two of his daughters were the handsomest Indian girls of full blood that I ever saw. His record as a councilor of his people and his policy in the new situation that confronted them was manly and consistent.

DULL KNIFE

THE life of Dull Knife, the Cheyenne, is a true hero tale. Simple, child-like yet manful, and devoid of self-ish aims, or love of gain, he is a pattern for heroes of any race.

Dull Knife was a chief of the old school. Among all the Indians of the plains, nothing counts save proven worth. A man's caliber is measured by his cour-age, unselfishness and intelligence. Many writers confuse history with fiction, but in Indian history their women and old men and even children witness the main events, and not being absorbed in daily papers and magazines, these events are rehearsed over and over with few vari-ations. Though orally preserved, their ac-counts are therefore accurate. But they have seldom been willing to give reliable

179

information to strangers, especially when asked and paid for.

Racial prejudice naturally enters into the account of a man's life by enemy writers, while one is likely to favor his own race. I am conscious that many readers may think that I have idealized the Indian. Therefore I will confess now that we have too many weak and unprincipled men among us. When I speak of the Indian hero, I do not forget the mongrel in spirit, false to the ideals of his people. Our trustfulness has been our weakness, and when the vices of civilization were added to our own, we fell heavily.

It is said that Dull Knife as a boy was resourceful and self-reliant. He was only nine years old when his family was separated from the rest of the tribe while on a buffalo hunt. His father was away and his mother busy, and he was playing with his little sister on the banks of a stream, when a large herd of buffalo swept down upon them on a stampede for water. His mother climbed a tree, but the little boy led his sister into an old beaver house whose entrance was above water, and here they remained in shelter until the buffalo passed and they were found by their distracted parents.

Dull Knife was quite a youth when his tribe was caught one winter in a region devoid of game, and threatened with starvation. The situation was made worse by heavy storms, but he secured help and led a relief party a hundred and fifty miles, carrying bales of dried buffalo meat on pack horses.

Another exploit that made him dear to his people occurred in battle, when his brother-in-law was severely wounded and left lying where no one on either side dared to approach him. As soon as Dull Knife heard of it he got on a fresh horse, and made so daring a charge that others joined him; thus under cover of their fire he rescued his brother-in-law, and in so doing was wounded twice.

The Sioux knew him as a man of high type, perhaps not so brilliant as Roman Nose and Two Moon, but surpassing both in honesty and simplicity, as well as in his war record. (Two Moon, in fact, was never a leader of his people, and became distinguished only in wars with the whites during the period of revolt.) A story is told of an ancestor of the same name that illustrates well the spirit of the age.

It was the custom in those days for the older men to walk ahead of the moving caravan and decide upon all halts and camping places. One day the councilors came to a grove of wild cherries covered with ripe fruit, and they stopped at once. Suddenly a grizzly charged from the thicket. The men yelped and hooted, but the bear was not to be bluffed. He knocked down the first warrior who dared to face him and dragged his victim into the bushes.

The whole caravan was in the wildest excitement. Several of the swiftest-footed warriors charged the bear, to bring him out into the open, while the women and dogs made all the noise they could. The bear accepted the challenge, and as he did so, the man whom they had supposed dead came running from the opposite end of the thicket. The Indians were delighted, and especially so when in the midst of their cheers, the man stopped running for his life and began to sing a Brave Heart song as he approached the grove with his butcher knife in his hand. He would dare his enemy again!

The grizzly met him with a tremendous rush, and they went down together. Instantly the bear began to utter cries of distress, and at the same time the knife flashed, and he rolled over dead. The warrior was too quick for the animal; he first bit his sensitive nose to distract his attention, and then used the knife to stab him to the heart. He fought many battles with knives thereafter and claimed that the spirit of the bear gave him suc-

cess. On one occasion, however, the enemy
had a strong buffalo-hide shield which the
Cheyenne bear fighter could not pierce
through, and he was wounded; nevertheless he managed to dispatch his foe. It
was from this incident that he received the
name of Dull Knife, which was handed down
to his descendant.

As is well known, the Northern Cheyennes uncompromisingly supported the
Sioux in their desperate defense of the
Black Hills and Big Horn country. Why
not? It was their last buffalo region —
their subsistence. It was what our wheat
fields are to a civilized nation.

About the year 1875, a propaganda was
started for confining all the Indians upon
reservations, where they would be practically interned or imprisoned, regardless
of their possessions and rights. The
men who were the strongest advocates of
the scheme generally wanted the Indians'
property — the one main cause back of all
Indian wars. From the warlike Apaches

to the peaceful Nez Perces, all the tribes of the plains were hunted from place to place; then the government resorted to peace negotiations, but always with an army at hand to coerce. Once disarmed and helpless, they were to be taken under military guard to the Indian Territory.

A few resisted, and declared they would fight to the death rather than go. Among these were the Sioux, but nearly all the smaller tribes were deported against their wishes. Of course those Indians who came from a mountainous and cold country suffered severely. The moist heat and malaria decimated the exiles. Chief Joseph of the Nez Perces and Chief Standing Bear of the Poncas appealed to the people of the United States, and finally succeeded in having their bands or the remnant of them returned to their own part of the country. Dull Knife was not successful in his plea, and the story of his flight is one of poignant interest.

He was regarded by the authorities as

a dangerous man, and with his depleted band was taken to the Indian Territory without his consent in 1876. When he realized that his people were dying like sheep, he was deeply moved. He called them together. Every man and woman declared that they would rather die in their own country than stay there longer, and they resolved to flee to their northern homes.

Here again was displayed the genius of these people. From the Indian Territory to Dakota is no short dash for freedom. They knew what they were facing. Their line of flight lay through a settled country and they would be closely pursued by the army. No sooner had they started than the telegraph wires sang one song: "The panther of the Cheyennes is at large. Not a child or a woman in Kansas or Nebraska is safe." Yet they evaded all the pursuing and intercepting troops and reached their native soil. The strain was terrible, the hardship great, and Dull

Knife, like Joseph, was remarkable for his self-restraint in sparing those who came within his power on the way.

But fate was against him, for there were those looking for blood money who betrayed him when he thought he was among friends. His people were tired out and famished when they were surrounded and taken to Fort Robinson. There the men were put in prison, and their wives guarded in camp. They were allowed to visit their men on certain days. Many of them had lost everything; there were but a few who had even one child left. They were heartbroken.

These despairing women appealed to their husbands to die fighting: their liberty was gone, their homes broken up, and only slavery and gradual extinction in sight. At last Dull Knife listened. He said: "I have lived my life. I am ready." The others agreed. "If our women are willing to die with us, who is there to say no? If we are to do the deeds of men, it rests with you women to bring us our weapons."

As they had been allowed to carry moccasins and other things to the men, so they contrived to take in some guns and knives under this disguise. The plan was to kill the sentinels and run to the nearest natural trench, there to make their last stand. The women and children were to join them. This arrangement was carried out. Not every brave had a gun, but all had agreed to die together. They fought till their small store of ammunition was exhausted, then exposed their broad chests for a target, and the mothers even held up their little ones to be shot. Thus died the fighting Cheyennes and their dauntless leader.

ROMAN NOSE

THIS Cheyenne war chief was a contemporary of Dull Knife. He was not so strong a character as the other, and was inclined to be pompous and boastful; but with all this he was a true type of native American in spirit and bravery.

While Dull Knife was noted in warfare among Indians, Roman Nose made his record against the whites, in defense of territory embracing the Republican and Arickaree rivers. He was killed on the latter river in 1868, in the celebrated battle with General Forsythe.

Save Chief Gall and Washakie in the prime of their manhood, this chief had no peer in bodily perfection and masterful personality. No Greek or Roman gymnast was ever a finer model of physical beauty and power. He thrilled his men to frenzied action when he came upon the field. It was said of him that he sacrificed more youths by his personal influence in battle than any other leader, being very reckless himself in grand-stand charges. He was killed needlessly in this manner.

Roman Nose always rode an uncommonly fine, spirited horse, and with his war bonnet and other paraphernalia gave a wonderful exhibition. The Indians used to say that the soldiers must gaze at him rather than aim at him, as they so seldom hit him even when running the gantlet before a firing line.

He did a remarkable thing once when on a one-arrow-to-kill buffalo hunt with his brother-in-law. His companion had selected his animal and drew so powerfully on his sinew bowstring that it broke. Roman Nose had killed his own cow and was whipping up close to the other when the misfortune occurred. Both horses were going at full speed and the arrow jerked up in the air. Roman Nose caught it and shot the cow for him.

Another curious story told of him is to the effect that he had an intimate Sioux friend who was courting a Cheyenne girl, but without success. As the wooing of both Sioux and Cheyennes was pretty much all effected in the night time, Roman Nose told his friend to let him do the courting for him. He arranged with the young woman to elope the next night and to spend the honeymoon among his Sioux friends. He then told his friend what to do. The Sioux followed instructions and carried off the Cheyenne maid, and not until morning did she discover her mistake. It is said she never admitted it, and that the two lived happily together to a good old age, so perhaps there was no mistake after all.

Perhaps no other chief attacked more emigrants going west on the Oregon Trail between 1860 and 1868. He once made an attack on a large party of Mormons, and in this instance the Mormons had time to form a corral with their wagons and shelter their women, children, and horses. The men stood outside and met the Indians with well-aimed volleys, but they circled the wagons with whirlwind speed, and whenever a white man fell, it was the signal for Roman Nose to charge and count the "coup." The hat of one of the dead men was off, and although he had heavy hair and beard, the top of his head was bald from the forehead up. As custom required such a deed to be announced on the spot, the chief yelled at the top of his voice:

"Your Roman Nose has counted the first coup on the longest-faced white man who was ever killed!"

When the Northern Cheyennes under this daring leader attacked a body of scouting troops under the brilliant officer General Forsythe, Roman Nose thought that he had a comparatively easy task. The first onset failed, and the command entrenched itself on a little island. The wily chief thought he could stampede them and urged on his braves with the declaration that the first to reach the island should be entitled to wear a trailing war bonnet. Nevertheless he was disappointed, and his men received such a warm reception that none succeeded in reaching it. In order to inspire them to desperate deeds he had led them in person, and with him that meant victory or death. According to the army accounts, it was a thrilling moment, and might well have proved disastrous to the Forsythe command, whose leader was wounded and helpless. The danger was acute until Roman Nose fell, and even then his lieutenants were bent upon crossing at any cost, but some of the older chiefs prevailed upon them to withdraw.

Thus the brilliant war chief of the Cheyennes came to his death. If he had lived until 1876, Sitting Bull would have had another bold ally.

CHIEF JOSEPH

THE Nez Perce tribe of Indians, like other tribes too large to be united under one chief, was composed of several bands, each distinct in sovereignty. It was a loose confederacy. Joseph and his people occupied the Imnaha or Grande Ronde valley in Oregon, which was considered perhaps the finest land in that part of the country.

When the last treaty was entered into by some of the bands of the Nez Perce, Joseph's band was at Lapwai, Idaho, and had nothing to do with the agreement. The elder chief in dying had counseled his son, then not more than twenty-two or twenty-three years of age, never to part with their home, assuring him that he had signed no papers. These peaceful non-treaty Indians did not even know what

land had been ceded until the agent read
them the government order to leave.   Of
course they refused. You and I would
have done the same.

When the agent failed to move them,
he and the would-be settlers called upon
the army to force them to be good, namely,
without a murmur to leave their pleasant
inheritance in the hands of a crowd of
greedy grafters. General O. O. Howard,
the Christian soldier, was sent to do the
work.

He had a long council with Joseph and
his leading men, telling them they must
obey the order or be driven out by force.
We may be sure that he presented this
hard alternative reluctantly. Joseph was
a mere youth without experience in war
or public affairs. He had been well brought
up in obedience to parental wisdom and
with his brother Ollicut had attended
Missionary Spaulding's school where they
had listened to the story of Christ and
his religion of brotherhood. He now re-

plied in his simple way that neither he nor
his father had ever made any treaty dis-
posing of their country, that no other
band of the Nez Perces was authorized to
speak for them, and it would seem a mighty
injustice and unkindness to dispossess a
friendly band.

General Howard told them in effect
that they had no rights, no voice in the
matter: they had only to obey. Although
some of the lesser chiefs counseled revolt
then and there, Joseph maintained his
self-control, seeking to calm his people,
and still groping for a peaceful settlement
of their difficulties. He finally asked for
thirty days' time in which to find and dis-
pose of their stock, and this was granted.

Joseph steadfastly held his immediate
followers to their promise, but the land-
grabbers were impatient, and did everything in their power to bring about an immediate crisis so as to hasten the eviction
of the Indians. Depredations were committed, and finally the Indians, or some of

them, retaliated, which was just what their
enemies had been looking for.   There might
be a score of white men murdered among
themselves on the frontier and no out-
sider would ever hear about it, but if one
were injured by an Indian — "Down with
the bloodthirsty savages!" was the cry.

Joseph told me himself that during all of
those thirty days a tremendous pressure
was brought upon him by his own people
to resist the government order. "The
worst of it was," said he, "that everything
they said was true; besides" — he paused
for a moment — "it seemed very soon for
me to forget my father's dying words, 'Do
not give up our home!'" Knowing as I
do just what this would mean to an Indian,
I felt for him deeply.

Among the opposition leaders were Too-
hul-hul-sote, White Bird, and Looking
Glass, all of them strong men and respected by the Indians; while on the
other side were men built up by emissaries
of the government for their own purposes

and advertised as "great friendly chiefs."
As a rule such men are unworthy, and this
is so well known to the Indians that it
makes them distrustful of the government's
sincerity at the start. Moreover, while
Indians unqualifiedly say what they mean,
the whites have a hundred ways of saying
what they do not mean.

The center of the storm was this simple
young man, who so far as I can learn had
never been upon the warpath, and he
stood firm for peace and obedience. As
for his father's sacred dying charge, he
told himself that he would not sign any
papers, he would not go of his free will
but from compulsion, and this was his
excuse.

However, the whites were unduly impatient to clear the coveted valley, and
by their insolence they aggravated to the
danger point an already strained situation.
The murder of an Indian was the climax,
and this happened in the absence of the
young chief. He returned to find the

leaders determined to die fighting. The nature of the country was in their favor and at least they could give the army a chase, but how long they could hold out they did not know. Even Joseph's younger brother Ollicut was won over. There was nothing for him to do but fight; and then and there began the peaceful Joseph's career as a general of unsurpassed strategy in conducting one of the most masterly retreats in history.

This is not my judgment, but the unbiased opinion of men whose knowledge and experience fit them to render it. Bear in mind that these people were not scalp hunters like the Sioux, Cheyennes, and Utes, but peaceful hunters and fishermen. The first council of war was a strange business to Joseph. He had only this to say to his people:

"I have tried to save you from suffering and sorrow. Resistance means all of that. We are few. They are many. You can see all we have at a glance. They have food and ammunition in abundance. We must suffer great hardship and loss." After this speech, he quietly began his plans for the defense.

The main plan of campaign was to engineer a successful retreat into Montana and there form a junction with the hostile Sioux and Cheyennes under Sitting Bull. There was a relay scouting system, one set of scouts leaving the main body at evening and the second a little before daybreak, passing the first set on some commanding hill top. There were also decoy scouts set to trap Indian scouts of the army. I notice that General Howard charges his Crow scouts with being unfaithful.

Their greatest difficulty was in meeting an unencumbered army, while carrying their women, children, and old men, with supplies and such household effects as were absolutely necessary. Joseph formed an auxiliary corps that was to effect a retreat at each engagement, upon a definite plan and in definite order, while the unencumbered women were made into an ambulance corps to take care of the wounded.

It was decided that the main rear guard should meet General Howard's command in White Bird Canyon, and every detail was planned in advance, yet left flexible according to Indian custom, giving each leader freedom to act according to circumstances. Perhaps no better ambush was ever planned than the one Chief Joseph set for the shrewd and experienced General Howard. He expected to be hotly pursued, but he calculated that the pursuing force would consist of not more than two hundred and fifty soldiers. He prepared false trails to mislead them into thinking that he was about to cross or had crossed the Salmon River, which he had no thought of doing at that time. Some of the tents were pitched in plain sight, while the women and children were hidden on the inaccessible ridges, and the men concealed in the canyon ready to fire upon the soldiers with deadly effect with scarcely any danger to themselves. They could even roll rocks upon them.

In a very few minutes the troops had learned a lesson. The soldiers showed some fight, but a large body of frontiersmen who accompanied them were soon in disorder. The warriors chased them nearly ten miles, securing rifles and much ammunition, and killing and wounding many.

The Nez Perces next crossed the river, made a detour and recrossed it at another point, then took their way eastward. All this was by way of delaying pursuit. Joseph told me that he estimated it would take six or seven days to get a sufficient force in the field to take up their trail, and the correctness of his reasoning is apparent from the facts as detailed in General Howard's book. He tells us that he waited six days for the arrival of men from various forts in his department, then followed Joseph with six hundred soldiers, beside a large number of citizen volunteers

and his Indian scouts. As it was evident
they had a long chase over trackless wilderness in prospect, he discarded his supply
wagons and took pack mules instead. But
by this time the Indians had a good start.

Meanwhile General Howard had sent a
dispatch to Colonel Gibbons, with orders
to head Joseph off, which he undertook to
do at the Montana end of the Lolo Trail.
The wily commander had no knowledge
of this move, but he was not to be surprised. He was too brainy for his pursuers, whom he constantly outwitted, and
only gave battle when he was ready.
There at the Big Hole Pass he met Colonel
Gibbons' fresh troops and pressed them
close. He sent a party under his brother
Ollicut to harass Gibbons' rear and rout
the pack mules, thus throwing him on the
defensive and causing him to send for help,
while Joseph continued his masterly retreat toward the Yellowstone Park, then
a wilderness. However, this was but little
advantage to him, since he must neces-

sarily leave a broad trail, and the army was
augmenting its columns day by day with
celebrated scouts, both white and Indian.
The two commands came together, and
although General Howard says their horses
were by this time worn out, and by in-
ference the men as well, they persisted on
the trail of a party encumbered by women
and children, the old, sick, and wounded.

It was decided to send a detachment of
cavalry under Bacon, to Tash Pass, the
gateway of the National Park, which
Joseph would have to pass, with orders to
detain him there until the rest could come
up with them. Here is what General
Howard says of the affair. "Bacon got
into position soon enough but he did not
have the heart to fight the Indians on
account of their number." Meanwhile another incident had occurred. Right under
the eyes of the chosen scouts and vigilant
sentinels, Joseph's warriors fired upon the
army camp at night and ran off their mules.
He went straight on toward the park,

where Lieutenant Bacon let him get by and pass through the narrow gateway without firing a shot.

Here again it was demonstrated that General Howard could not depend upon the volunteers, many of whom had joined him in the chase, and were going to show the soldiers how to fight Indians. In this night attack at Camas Meadow, they were demoralized, and while crossing the river next day many lost their guns in the water, whereupon all packed up and went home, leaving the army to be guided by the Indian scouts.

However, this succession of defeats did not discourage General Howard, who kept on with as many of his men as were able to carry a gun, meanwhile sending dispatches to all the frontier posts with orders to intercept Joseph if possible. Sturgis tried to stop him as the Indians entered the Park, but they did not meet until he was about to come out, when there was another fight, with Joseph again victorious.

General Howard came upon the battle
field soon afterward and saw that the
Indians were off again, and from here he
sent fresh messages to General Miles, asking for reinforcements.

Joseph had now turned northeastward
toward the Upper Missouri. He told me
that when he got into that part of the
country he knew he was very near the
Canadian line and could not be far from
Sitting Bull, with whom he desired to form
an alliance. He also believed that he had
cleared all the forts. Therefore he went
more slowly and tried to give his people
some rest. Some of their best men had
been killed or wounded in battle, and the
wounded were a great burden to him;
nevertheless they were carried and tended
patiently all during this wonderful flight.
Not one was ever left behind.

It is the general belief that Indians are
cruel and revengeful, and surely these
people had reason to hate the race who
had driven them from their homes if any

CHIEF JOSEPH

people ever had. Yet it is a fact that
when Joseph met visitors and travelers in
the Park, some of whom were women, he
allowed them to pass unharmed, and in
at least one instance let them have horses.
He told me that he gave strict orders to
his men not to kill any women or children.
He wished to meet his adversaries according to their own standards of warfare, but
he afterward learned that in spite of pro-
fessions of humanity, white soldiers have
not seldom been known to kill women and
children indiscriminately.

Another remarkable thing about this
noted retreat is that Joseph's people stood
behind him to a man, and even the women
and little boys did each his part. The
latter were used as scouts in the immediate
vicinity of the camp.

The Bittersweet valley, which they had
now entered, was full of game, and the
Indians hunted for food, while resting their
worn-out ponies. One morning they had
a council to which Joseph rode over bare-

back, as they had camped in two divisions a little apart. His fifteen-year-old daughter went with him. They discussed sending runners to Sitting Bull to ascertain his exact whereabouts and whether it would be agreeable to him to join forces with the Nez Perces. In the midst of the council, a force of United States cavalry charged down the hill between the two camps. This once Joseph was surprised. He had seen no trace of the soldiers and had somewhat relaxed his vigilance.

He told his little daughter to stay where she was, and himself cut right through the cavalry and rode up to his own teepee, where his wife met him at the door with his rifle, crying: "Here is your gun, husband!" The warriors quickly gathered and pressed the soldiers so hard that they had to withdraw. Meanwhile one set of the people fled while Joseph's own band intrenched themselves in a very favorable position from which they could not easily be dislodged.

General Miles had received and acted on General Howard's message, and he now sent one of his officers with some Indian scouts into Joseph's camp to negotiate with the chief. Meantime Howard and Sturgis came up with the encampment, and Howard had with him two friendly Nez Perce scouts who were directed to talk to Joseph in his own language. He decided that there was nothing to do but surrender.

He had believed that his escape was all but secure: then at the last moment he was surprised and caught at a disadvantage. His army was shattered; he had lost most of the leaders in these various fights; his people, including children, women, and the wounded, had traveled thirteen hundred miles in about fifty days, and he himself a young man who had never before taken any important responsibility! Even now he was not actually conquered. He was well intrenched; his people were willing to die fighting; but the army of

the United States offered peace and he
agreed, as he said, out of pity for his suffering people. Some of his warriors still
refused to surrender and slipped out of the
camp at night and through the lines.
Joseph had, as he told me, between three
and four hundred fighting men in the beginning, which means over one thousand
persons, and of these several hundred surrendered with him.

His own story of the conditions he
made was prepared by himself with my
help in 1897, when he came to Washington to present his grievances. I sat up
with him nearly all of one night; and I
may add here that we took the document
to General Miles who was then stationed
in Washington, before presenting it to the
Department. The General said that every
word of it was true.

In the first place, his people were to be
kept at Fort Keogh, Montana, over the
winter and then returned to their reservation. Instead they were taken to Fort

Leavenworth, Kansas, and placed between
a lagoon and the Missouri River, where
the sanitary conditions made havoc with
them. Those who did not die were then
taken to the Indian Territory, where the
health situation was even worse. Joseph
appealed to the government again and
again, and at last by the help of Bishops
Whipple and Hare he was moved to the
Colville reservation in Washington. Here
the land was very poor, unlike their own
fertile valley. General Miles said to the
chief that he had recommended and urged
that their agreement be kept, but the
politicians and the people who occupied
the Indians' land declared they were afraid
if he returned he would break out again
and murder innocent white settlers! What
irony!

The great Chief Joseph died broken-
spirited and broken-hearted. He did
not hate the whites, for there was nothing small about him, and when he laid
down his weapons he would not fight on

with his mind. But he was profoundly
disappointed in the claims of a Christian
civilization. I call him great because he
was simple and honest. Without education
or special training he demonstrated his
ability to lead and to fight when justice
demanded. He outgeneraled the best and
most experienced commanders in the army
of the United States, although their troops
were well provisioned, well armed, and
above all unencumbered. He was great
finally, because he never boasted of his
remarkable feat. I am proud of him, because he was a true American.

LITTLE WOLF

IF any people ever fought for liberty and justice, it was the Cheyennes. If any ever demonstrated their physical and moral courage beyond cavil, it was this race of purely American heroes, among whom Little Wolf was a leader.

I knew the chief personally very well. As a young doctor, I was sent to the Pine Ridge agency in 1890, as government physician to the Sioux and the Northern Cheyennes. While I heard from his own lips of that gallant dash of his people from their southern exile to their northern home, I prefer that Americans should read of it in Doctor George Bird Grinnell's book, "The Fighting Cheyennes." No account could be clearer or simpler; and then too, the author cannot be charged with a bias in favor of his own race.

At the time that I knew him, Little Wolf was a handsome man, with the native dignity and gentleness, musical voice, and pleasant address of so many brave leaders of his people. One day when he was dining with us at our home on the reservation, I asked him, as I had a habit of doing, for some reminiscences of his early life. He was rather reluctant to speak, but a friend who was present contributed the following:

"Perhaps I can tell you why it is that he has been a lucky man all his life. When quite a small boy, the tribe was one winter in want of food, and his good mother had saved a small piece of buffalo meat, which she solemnly brought forth and placed before him with the remark: 'My son must be patient, for when he grows up he will know even harder times than this.'

"He had eaten nothing all day and was pretty hungry, but before he could lay hands on the meat a starving dog snatched it and bolted from the teepee. The mother ran after the dog and brought him back for punishment. She tied him to a post and was about to whip him when the boy interfered. 'Don't hurt him, mother!' he cried; 'he took the meat because he was hungrier than I am!'"

I was told of another kind act of his under trying circumstances. While still a youth, he was caught out with a party of buffalo hunters in a blinding blizzard. They were compelled to lie down side by side in the snowdrifts, and it was a day and a night before they could get out. The weather turned very cold, and when the men arose they were in danger of freezing. Little Wolf pressed his fine buffalo robe upon an old man who was shaking with a chill and himself took the other's thin blanket.

As a full-grown young man, he was attracted by a maiden of his tribe, and according to the custom then in vogue the pair disappeared. When they returned to the camp as man and wife, behold! there was great excitement over the affair. It seemed that a certain chief had given many presents and paid unmistakable court to the maid with the intention of marrying her, and her parents had accepted the presents, which meant consent so far as they were concerned. But the girl herself had not given consent.

The resentment of the disappointed suitor was great. It was reported in the village that he had openly declared that the young man who defied and insulted him must expect to be punished. As soon as Little Wolf heard of the threats, he told his father and friends that he had done only what it is every man's privilege to do.

"Tell the chief," said he, "to come out with any weapon he pleases, and I will meet him within the circle of lodges. He shall either do this or eat his words. The woman is not his. Her people accepted his gifts against her wishes. Her heart is mine."

The chief apologized, and thus avoided the inevitable duel, which would have been a fight to the death.

The early life of Little Wolf offered many examples of the dashing bravery characteristic of the Cheyennes, and inspired the younger men to win laurels for themselves. He was still a young man, perhaps thirty-five, when the most trying crisis in the history of his people came upon them. As I know and as Doctor Grinnell's book amply corroborates, he was the general who largely guided and defended them in that tragic flight from the Indian Territory to their northern home. I will not discuss the justice of their cause: I prefer to quote Doctor Grinnell, lest it appear that I am in any way exaggerating the facts.

"They had come," he writes, "from the high, dry country of Montana and North Dakota to the hot and humid Indian Territory. They had come from a country where buffalo and other game were still plentiful to a land where the game had been exterminated. Immediately on their arrival they were attacked by fever and ague, a disease wholly new to them. Food was scanty, and they began to starve. The agent testified before a committee of the Senate that he never received supplies to subsist the Indians for more than nine months in each year. These people were meat-eaters, but the beef furnished them by the government inspectors was no more than skin and bone. The agent in describing their sufferings said: 'They have lived and that is about all.'

"The Indians endured this for about a year, and then their patience gave out. They left the agency to which they had been sent and started north. Though troops were camped close to them, they attempted no concealment of their purpose. Instead, they openly announced that they intended to return to their own country.

"We have heard much in past years of

the march of the Nez Perces under Chief
Joseph, but little is remembered of the
Dull Knife outbreak and the march to the
north led by Little Wolf. The story of
the journey has not been told, but in the
traditions of the old army this campaign
was notable, and old men who were stationed on the plains forty years ago are
apt to tell you, if you ask them, that there
never was such another journey since the
Greeks marched to the sea. . . .

"The fugitives pressed constantly northward undaunted, while orders were flying
over the wires, and special trains were
carrying men and horses to cut them off
at all probable points on the different
railway lines they must cross. Of the
three hundred Indians, sixty or seventy
were fighting men — the rest old men,
women, and children. An army officer
once told me that thirteen thousand troops
were hurrying over the country to capture
or kill these few poor people who had left
the fever-stricken South, and in the face

of every obstacle were steadily marching northward.

"The War Department set all its resources in operation against them, yet they kept on. If troops attacked them, they stopped and fought until they had driven off the soldiers, and then started north again. Sometimes they did not even stop, but marched along, fighting as they marched. For the most part they tried — and with success — to avoid conflicts, and had but four real hard fights, in which they lost half a dozen men killed and about as many wounded."

It must not be overlooked that the appeal to justice had first been tried before taking this desperate step. Little Wolf had gone to the agent about the middle of the summer and said to him: "This is not a good country for us, and we wish to return to our home in the mountains where we were always well. If you have not the power to give permission, let some of us go to Washington and tell them there

how it is, or do you write to Washington
and get permission for us to go back."

"Stay one more year," replied the agent,
"and then we will see what we can do for
you." "No," said Little Wolf. "Before
another year there will be none left to
travel north. We must go now."

Soon after this it was found that three
of the Indians had disappeared and the
chief was ordered to surrender ten men as
hostages for their return. He refused.
"Three men," said he, "who are traveling
over wild country can hide so that they
cannot be found. You would never get
back these three, and you would keep my
men prisoners always."

The agent then threatened if the ten
men were not given up to withhold their
rations and starve the entire tribe into submission. He forgot that he was address-
ing a Cheyenne. These people had not
understood that they were prisoners when
they agreed to friendly relations with the
government and came upon the reserva-

tion. Little Wolf stood up and shook
hands with all present before making his
final deliberate address.

"Listen, my friends, I am a friend of
the white people and have been so for a
long time. I do not want to see blood spilt
about this agency. I am going north to
my own country. If you are going to
send your soldiers after me, I wish you
would let us get a little distance away.
Then if you want to fight, I will fight you,
and we can make the ground bloody at
that place."

The Cheyenne was not bluffing. He
said just what he meant, and I presume
the agent took the hint, for although the
military were there they did not undertake to prevent the Indians' departure.
Next morning the teepees were pulled
down early and quickly. Toward evening
of the second day, the scouts signaled the
approach of troops. Little Wolf called
his men together and advised them under
no circumstances to fire until fired upon.

LITTLE WOLF

An Arapahoe scout was sent to them with
a message. "If you surrender now, you
will get your rations and be well treated."
After what they had endured, it was impossible not to hear such a promise with
contempt. Said Little Wolf: "We are
going back to our own country. We do
not want to fight." He was riding still
nearer when the soldiers fired, and at a
signal the Cheyennes made a charge.
They succeeded in holding off the troops
for two days, with only five men wounded
and none killed, and when the military retreated the Indians continued northward
carrying their wounded.

This sort of thing was repeated again
and again. Meanwhile Little Wolf held
his men under perfect control. There were
practically no depredations. They secured
some boxes of ammunition left behind by
retreating troops, and at one point the
young men were eager to follow and destroy an entire command who were apparently at their mercy, but their leader

withheld them. They had now reached the buffalo country, and he always kept his main object in sight. He was extraordinarily calm. Doctor Grinnell was told by one of his men years afterward: "Little Wolf did not seem like a human being. He seemed like a bear." It is true that a man of his type in a crisis becomes spiritually transformed and moves as one in a dream.

At the Running Water the band divided, Dull Knife going toward Red Cloud agency. He was near Fort Robinson when he surrendered and met his sad fate. Little Wolf remained all winter in the Sand Hills, where there was plenty of game and no white men. Later he went to Montana and then to Pine Ridge, where he and his people remained in peace until they were removed to Lame Deer, Montana, and there he spent the remainder of his days. There is a clear sky beyond the clouds of racial prejudice, and in that final Court of Honor a noble soul like that of Little Wolf has a place.

HOLE-IN-THE-DAY [1]

IN the beginning of the nineteenth century, the Indian nations of the Northwest first experienced the pressure of civilization. At this period there were among them some brilliant leaders unknown to history, for the curious reason that they cordially received and welcomed the newcomers rather than opposed them. The only difficulties were those arising among the European nations themselves, and often involving the native tribes. Thus new environments brought new motives, and our temptations were increased manyfold with the new weapons, new goods, and above all the subtly destructive "spirit water."

Gradually it became known that the new race had a definite purpose, and that

[1] I wish to thank Reverend C. H. Beaulieu of Le Soeur, Minnesota, for much of the material used in this chapter.

purpose was to chart and possess the whole country, regardless of the rights of its earlier inhabitants. Still the old chiefs cautioned their people to be patient, for, said they, the land is vast, both races can live on it, each in their own way. Let us therefore befriend them and trust to their friendship. While they reasoned thus, the temptations of graft and self-aggrandizement overtook some of the leaders.

Hole-in-the-Day (or Bug-o-nay-ki-shig) was born in the opening days of this era. The word "ki-shig" means either "day" or "sky", and the name is perhaps more correctly translated Hole-in-the-Sky. This gifted man inherited his name and much of his ability from his father, who was a war chief among the Ojibways, a Napoleon of the common people, and who carried on a relentless warfare against the Sioux. And yet, as was our custom at the time, peaceful meetings were held every summer, at which representatives of the two tribes would recount to one another all

the events that had come to pass during
the preceding year.

Hole-in-the-Day the younger was a
handsome man, tall and symmetrically
formed, with much grace of manner and
natural refinement. He was an astute
student of diplomacy. The Ojibways allowed polygamy, and whether or not he
approved the principle, he made political
use of it by marrying the daughter of a
chief in nearly every band. Through these
alliances he held a controlling influence
over the whole Ojibway nation. Reverend
Claude H. Beaulieu says of him:

"Hole-in-the-Day was a man of distinguished appearance and native courtli-
ness of manner. His voice was musical
and magnetic, and with these qualities
he had a subtle brain, a logical mind, and
quite a remarkable gift of oratory. In
speech he was not impassioned, but clear
and convincing, and held fast the attention of his hearers."

It is of interest to note that his every-

day name among his tribesmen was "The
Boy." What a boy he must have been!
I wonder if the name had the same sig-
nificance as with the Sioux, who applied
it to any man who performs a difficult duty
with alertness, dash, and natural courage.
"The Man" applies to one who adds to
these qualities wisdom and maturity of
judgment.

The Sioux tell many stories of both the
elder and the younger Hole-in-the-Day.
Once when The Boy was still under ten
years of age, he was fishing on Gull Lake
in a leaky birch-bark canoe. Presently
there came such a burst of frantic war
whoops that his father was startled. He
could not think of anything but an attack
by the dreaded Sioux. Seizing his weapons,
he ran to the rescue of his son, only to
find that the little fellow had caught a
fish so large that it was pulling his canoe
all over the lake. "Ugh," exclaimed the
father, "if a mere fish scares you so badly,
I fear you will never make a warrior!"

It is told of him that when he was very small, the father once brought home two bear cubs and gave them to him for pets. The Boy was feeding and getting acquainted with them outside his mother's birch-bark teepee, when suddenly he was heard to yell for help. The two little bears had treed The Boy and were waltzing around the tree. His mother scared them off, but again the father laughed at him for thinking that he could climb trees better than a bear.

The elder Hole-in-the-Day was a daring warrior and once attacked and scalped a Sioux who was carrying his pelts to the trading post, in full sight of his friends. Of course he was instantly pursued, and he leaped into a canoe which was lying near by and crossed to an island in the Mississippi River near Fort Snelling. When almost surrounded by Sioux warriors, he left the canoe and swam along the shore with only his nose above water, but as they were about to head him off he

landed and hid behind the falling sheet
of water known as Minnehaha Falls, thus
saving his life.

It often happens that one who offers his
life freely will after all die a natural death.
The elder Hole-in-the-Day so died when
The Boy was still a youth. Like Philip
of Massachusetts, Chief Joseph the
younger, and the brilliant Osceola, the
mantle fell gracefully upon his shoulders,
and he wore it during a short but event-
ful term of chieftainship. It was his to
see the end of the original democracy on
this continent. The clouds were fast
thickening on the eastern horizon. The
day of individualism and equity between
man and man must yield to the terrific
forces of civilization, the mass play of
materialism, the cupidity of commerce
with its twin brother politics. Under such
conditions the younger Hole-in-the-Day
undertook to guide his tribesmen. At
first they were inclined to doubt the wisdom of so young a leader, but he soon

proved a ready student of his people's traditions, and yet, like Spotted Tail and Little Crow, he adopted too willingly the white man's politics. He maintained the territory won from the Sioux by his predecessors. He negotiated treaties with the ability of a born diplomat, with one exception, and that exception cost him his life.

Like other able Indians who foresaw the inevitable downfall of their race, he favored a gradual change of customs leading to complete adoption of the white man's ways. In order to accustom the people to a new standard, he held that the chiefs must have authority and must be given compensation for their services. This was a serious departure from the old rule but was tacitly accepted, and in every treaty he made there was provision for himself in the way of a land grant or a cash payment. He early departed from the old idea of joint ownership with the Lake Superior Ojibways, because he foresaw that it would cause no end of trouble for

the Mississippi River branch of which he
was then the recognized head. But there
were difficulties to come with the Leech
Lake and Red Lake bands, who held
aloof from his policy, and the question of
boundaries began to arise.

In the first treaty negotiated with the
government by young Hole-in-the-Day in
1855, a "surplus" was provided for the
chiefs aside from the regular per capita
payment, and this surplus was to be dis-
tributed in proportion to the number of
Indians under each. Hole-in-the-Day had
by far the largest enrollment, therefore he
got the lion's share of this fund. Furthermore he received another sum set apart
for the use of the "head chief", and these
things did not look right to the tribe. In
the very next treaty he provided himself
with an annuity of one thousand dollars
for twenty years, beside a section of land
near the village of Crow Wing, and the
government was induced to build him a
good house upon this land. In his home

he had many white servants and hench-
men and really lived like a lord. He
dressed well in native style with a touch
of civilized elegance, wearing coat and
leggings of fine broadcloth, linen shirt
with collar, and, topping all, a handsome
black or blue blanket. His moccasins were
of the finest deerskin and beautifully
worked. His long beautiful hair added
much to his personal appearance. He was
fond of entertaining and being entertained
and was a favorite both among army
officers and civilians. He was especially
popular with the ladies, and this fact will
appear later in the story.

At about this time, the United States
government took it upon itself to put an
end to warfare between the Sioux and
Ojibways. A peace meeting was arranged
at Fort Snelling, with the United States
as mediator. When the representatives of
the two nations met at this grand council,
Hole-in-the-Day came as the head chief
of his people, and with the other chiefs

appeared in considerable pomp and dignity. The wives of the government officials were eager for admission to this
unusual gathering, but when they arrived
there was hardly any space left except next
to the Sioux chiefs, and the white ladies
soon crowded this space to overflowing.
One of the Sioux remarked: "I thought
this was to be a council of chiefs and
braves, but I see many women among us."
Thereupon the Ojibway arose and spoke
in his courtliest manner. "The Ojibway
chiefs will feel highly honored," said he,
"if the ladies will consent to sit on our side."

Another sign of his alertness to gain
favor among the whites was seen in the
fact that he took part in the territorial
campaigns, a most unusual thing for an
Indian of that day. Being a man of
means and influence, he was listened to
with respect by the scattered white settlers in his vicinity. He would make a
political speech through an interpreter,
but would occasionally break loose in his

broken English, and wind up with an invitation to drink in the following words:
"Chentimen, you Pemicans (Republicans),
come out and drink!"

From 1855 to 1864 Hole-in-the-Day was
a well-known figure in Minnesota, and
scarcely less so in Washington, for he
visited the capital quite often on tribal
affairs. As I have said before, he was an
unusually handsome man, and was not
unresponsive to flattery and the attentions
of women. At the time of this incident
he was perhaps thirty-five years old, but
looked younger. He had called upon the
President and was on his way back to his
hotel, when he happened to pass the
Treasury building just as the clerks were
leaving for the day. He was immediately
surrounded by an inquisitive throng.
Among them was a handsome young
woman who asked through the interpreter
if the chief would consent to an interview
about his people, to aid her in a paper she
had promised to prepare.

Hole-in-the-Day replied: "If the beautiful lady is willing to risk calling on the chief at his hotel, her request will be granted." The lady went, and the result was so sudden and strong an attachment that both forgot all racial biases and differences of language and custom. She followed him as far as Minneapolis, and there the chief advised her to remain, for he feared the jealousy of some of his many wives. She died there, soon after giving birth to a son, who was brought up by a family named Woodbury; and some fifteen years ago I met the young man in Washington and was taken by him to call upon certain of his mother's relatives.

The ascendancy of Hole-in-the-Day was not gained entirely through the consent of his people, but largely by government favor, therefore there was strong suppressed resentment among his associate chiefs, and the Red Lake and Leech Lake bands in fact never acknowledged him as their head, while they suspected him of

making treaties which involved some of
their land. He was in personal danger
from this source, and his life was twice
attempted, but, though wounded, in each
case he recovered. His popularity with
Indian agents and officers lasted till the
Republicans came into power in the sixties
and there was a new deal. The chief no
longer received the favors and tips to which
he was accustomed; in fact he was in
want of luxuries, and worse still, his pride
was hurt by neglect. The new party had
promised Christian treatment to the Indians, but it appeared that they were
greater grafters than their predecessors,
and unlike them kept everything for themselves, allowing no perquisites to any Indian chief.

In his indignation at this treatment,
Hole-in-the-Day began exposing the frauds
on his people, and so at a late day was
converted to their defense. Perhaps he
had not fully understood the nature of
graft until he was in a position to view it

from the outside. After all, he was ex-
cusable in seeking to maintain the dignity
of his office, but he had departed from one
of the fundamental rules of the race,
namely: "Let no material gain be the
motive or reward of public duty." He
had wounded the ideals of his people beyond forgiveness, and he suffered the pen-
alty; yet his courage was not diminished
by the mistakes of his past. Like the
Sioux chief Little Crow, he was called
"the betrayer of his people", and like him
he made a desperate effort to regain lost
prestige, and turned savagely against the
original betrayers of his confidence, the
agents and Indian traders.

When the Sioux finally broke out in
1862, the first thought of the local politicians was to humiliate Hole-in-the-Day
by arresting him and proclaiming some
other "head chief" in his stead. In so
doing they almost forced the Ojibways to
fight under his leadership. The chief had
no thought of alliance with the Sioux, and

was wholly unaware of the proposed action of the military on pretense of such a conspiracy on his part. He was on his way to the agency in his own carriage when a runner warned him of his danger. He thereupon jumped down and instructed the driver to proceed. His coachman was arrested by a file of soldiers, who when they discovered their mistake went to his residence in search of him, but meanwhile he had sent runners in every direction to notify his warriors, and had moved his family across the Mississippi. When the military reached the river bank he was still in sight, and the lieutenant called upon him to surrender. When he refused, the soldiers were ordered to fire upon him, but he replied with his own rifle, and with a whoop disappeared among the pine groves.

It was remarkable how the whole tribe now rallied to the call of Hole-in-the-Day. He allowed no depredations to the young men under his leadership, but camped openly near the agency and awaited an explanation. Presently Judge Cooper of St. Paul, a personal friend of the chief, appeared, and later on the Assistant Secretary of the Interior, accompanied by Mr. Nicolay, private secretary of President Lincoln. Apparently that great humanitarian President saw the whole injustice of the proceeding against a loyal nation, and the difficulty was at an end.

Through the treaties of 1864, 1867, and 1868 was accomplished the final destiny of the Mississippi River Ojibways. Hole-in-the-Day was against their removal to what is now White Earth reservation, but he was defeated in this and realized that the new turn of events meant the downfall of his race. He declared that he would never go on the new reservation, and he kept his word. He remained on one of his land grants near Crow Wing. As the other chiefs assumed more power, the old feeling of suspicion and hatred became stronger, especially among the Pillager and Red Lake bands. One day he was waylaid and shot by a party of these disaffected Indians. He uttered a whoop and fell dead from his buggy.

Thus died one of the most brilliant chiefs of the Northwest, who never defended his birthright by force of arms, although almost compelled to do so. He succeeded in diplomacy so long as he was the recognized head of his people. Since we have not passed over his weaknesses, he should be given credit for much insight in causing the article prohibiting the introduction of liquor into the Indian country to be inserted into the treaty of 1858. I think it was in 1910 that this forgotten provision was discovered and again enforced over a large expanse of territory occupied by whites, it being found that the provision had never been repealed.

Although he left many children, none seem to have made their mark, yet it may be that in one of his descendants that undaunted spirit will rise again.

Other Books by Charles A. Eastman
Available in Bison Book Editions

From the Deep Woods to Civilization:
Chapters in the Autobiography of an Indian

Old Indian Days

The Soul of the Indian: An Interpretation

Wigwam Evenings: Sioux Folk Tales Retold
(with Elaine Goodale Eastman)